Vertebrate inventory of Hagerman Fossil Beds National Monument 2003

Upper Columbia Basin Network

Natural Resource Technical Report NPS/UCBN/NRTR — 2010/297

Katherine Oelrich
University of Idaho
Department of Fish and Wildlife Resources
Moscow, Idaho 83844-1136

Thomas J. Rodhouse
National Park Service, Upper Columbia Basin Network
Central Oregon Community College, 2600 NW College Way – Ponderosa Building
Bend, Oregon 97701-5998

Lisa K. Garrett
National Park Service, Upper Columbia Basin Network
University of Idaho, Department of Fish and Wildlife
Moscow, Idaho 83844-1136

March 2010

U.S. Department of the Interior
National Park Service
Natural Resource Program Center
Fort Collins, Colorado

The National Park Service, Natural Resource Program Center publishes a range of reports that address natural resource topics of interest and applicability to a broad audience in the National Park Service and others in natural resource management, including scientists, conservation and environmental constituencies, and the public.

The Natural Resource Technical Report Series is used to disseminate results of scientific studies in the physical, biological, and social sciences for both the advancement of science and the achievement of the National Park Service mission. The series provides contributors with a forum for displaying comprehensive data that are often deleted from journals because of page limitations.

All manuscripts in the series receive the appropriate level of peer review to ensure that the information is scientifically credible, technically accurate, appropriately written for the intended audience, and designed and published in a professional manner. This report received formal peer review by subject-matter experts who were not directly involved in the collection, analysis, or reporting of the data, and whose background and expertise put them on par technically and scientifically with the authors of the information.

Views, statements, findings, conclusions, recommendations, and data in this report are those of the author(s) and do not necessarily reflect views and policies of the National Park Service, U.S. Department of the Interior. Mention of trade names or commercial products does not constitute endorsement or recommendation for use by the National Park Service.

This report is available from the Upper Columbia Basin Network website (http://www.nature.nps.gov/im/units/UCBN) and the Natural Resource Publications Management website (http://www.nature.nps.gov/publications/NRPM).

Please cite this publication as:

NPS 300/101467, March 2010

Contents

Contents

Figures

Tables

Appendices

Executive Summary

The 2003 Hagerman Fossil Beds National Monument vertebrate inventory developed species lists and additional information on birds, non-volant mammals, and herpetofauna in the Hagerman Fossil Beds of south central Idaho. Bats were not included in the 2003 vertebrate inventory. The University of Idaho Department of Fish and Wildlife Resources conducted the 2003 inventory under a cooperative agreement with the National Park Service Upper Columbia Basin Network in partial fulfillment of the Natural Resource Challenge Inventory and Monitoring Program. The primary goal of the inventory was to confirm 90% of the species expected to occur in the monument. Additional goals include developing baseline data for monitoring as well as providing the National Park Service and the research community-at-large with new and important information on the biodiversity of the region.

Expected species lists were developed from available historic sources and expert opinion. A set of four criteria was used to determine the likelihood of detection in the monument. Fieldwork in 2003 utilized a variety of methods to achieve the primary objective, including visual encounter surveys and trapping. Species documentation included the collection of voucher photographs, specimens, and field observation records. A 2001 field visit from the University of Idaho was included in the 2003 results. Recent results from the Hagerman Valley Christmas Bird Count and bird species confirmations from the nearby Thousand Springs Nature Conservancy reserve were also used to confirm species presence. The 2003 inventory was productive and brought species confirmation totals to 99% for birds, 79% for mammals, and 78% for amphibians and reptiles. One hundred fifty-four birds were expected to occur in or near the monument and 153 expected species are confirmed as well as 41 additional species that were not expected to occur. Thirty-three species of mammals were expected in the monument during 2003. Twenty-six were confirmed. One of these species, the white-tailed antelope ground squirrel (*Ammospermophilus leucurus*) was not expected to occur in the monument. The pronghorn (*Antilocapra americana*) was confirmed in one location just outside of the monument. Of the 18 expected species of herpetofauna, 14 species were confirmed. A total of 4 amphibians and 10 reptiles were documented on the monument. The Sagebrush Lizard (*Sceloporus graciosus*) was found in one discrete location in the monument in 2003.

Data from the 2003 inventory is incorporated into a long-term monitoring program that focuses on selected "vital-signs". Future monitoring activities will also provide opportunities to add additional species to the inventory list as they are encountered.

Acknowledgements

The 2003 Hagerman Fossil Beds National Monument vertebrate inventory was made possible through an agreement between the National Park Service Upper Columbia Basin Inventory and Monitoring Network and University of Idaho Department of Fish and Wildlife Resources. We would like to extend a special thanks to Dr. Gerry Wright, USGS Idaho Cooperative Wildlife Research Unit, and Fran Gruchy, Chief of Operations for the Hagerman Fossil Beds National Monument for providing leadership, direction, and enthusiasm for the project. Phil Gensler, monument paleontologist, provided valuable support and shared natural history sightings and information. Special thanks go to Kelly Wild of Idaho Power for the use of herpetological field equipment. Dr. John Cossel Jr. and Northwest Nazarene University deserves special thanks for all of the assistance and support. Dr. Charles Peterson, Idaho State University herpetologist, provided assistance in sampling design and expected herpetofauna. Sarah Harris and the Hagerman Valley Christmas Bird Count provided invaluable assistance with expected and confirmed birds in and adjacent to the monument. Kent Fothergill supplied recent bird sightings and provided information on the abundance and residency status of birds.

Introduction

This report summarizes the results of the 2003 inventory of birds, mammals, and herpetofauna, summarizes historic information, and contains brief accounts of each species present or expected to occur in the Hagerman Fossil Beds National Monument (HAFO). Information on species that are possible but unlikely to occur in the monument is also included.

The 2003 vertebrate inventory was conducted in the Hagerman Fossil Beds NM by the University of Idaho Department of Fish and Wildlife Resources under a cooperative agreement with the National Park Service Upper Columbia Basin Network. The inventory is part of a nationwide inventory and monitoring (I & M) program initiated by the National Park Service Natural Resource Challenge. In 2000, the Upper Columbia Basin Network, which includes Hagerman Fossil Beds National Monument, began implementing the inventory phase of the I & M program in several of the network parks and monuments. Historic information available on the plant and animal populations within the network were assembled and an estimate was made of the percent of species expected to occur in each park. Hagerman Fossil Beds was among the majority of network parks that had a low percentage (below 50%) of confirmed species of vertebrates and was in need of a concerted effort to meet the I & M goals.

The primary goal of the inventory phase of the I & M program was to document the presence of 90% of the plant and animal species expected to occur within the park boundary or within a distance to the boundary that is relevant to the biology of the organism and to park management. Secondary goals of the inventory included providing baseline information to help guide the development of the I & M program's vital signs monitoring strategy. Tertiary goals included providing both the NPS and the research community–at-large with new information on the distribution, habitat association, and population status of the nation's biological resources. Ultimately, the I & M program is designed to help the NPS take a leading role in the preservation of the nation's biodiversity. Completing basic biological inventories is a crucial first step in achieving that goal.

Study Area

The Hagerman Fossil Beds National Monument is located in the Snake River Valley in southern Idaho. Paleontologists from the Smithsonian Institute in 1929 made the first excavations at the Hagerman Fossil Beds. The monument was established in 1988 and the congressional boundaries include a total of 4,281 acres. Hagerman Fossil Beds is located in Gooding County and Twin Falls County. The monument headquarters are found in the city of Hagerman. Ownership patterns adjacent to the monument consist of a mosaic of Bureau of Land Management (BLM) and private lands, and this ownership pattern is influential in the biological diversity of the monument. There are also several parks and wildlife refuges near the fossil beds, including Malad Gorge State Park, Billingsley Creek State Wildlife Management Area, Thousand Springs Nature Conservancy Reserve, and Hagerman Wildlife Management Area. Figures 1 and 2 show maps of the northern and southern portions of the monument.

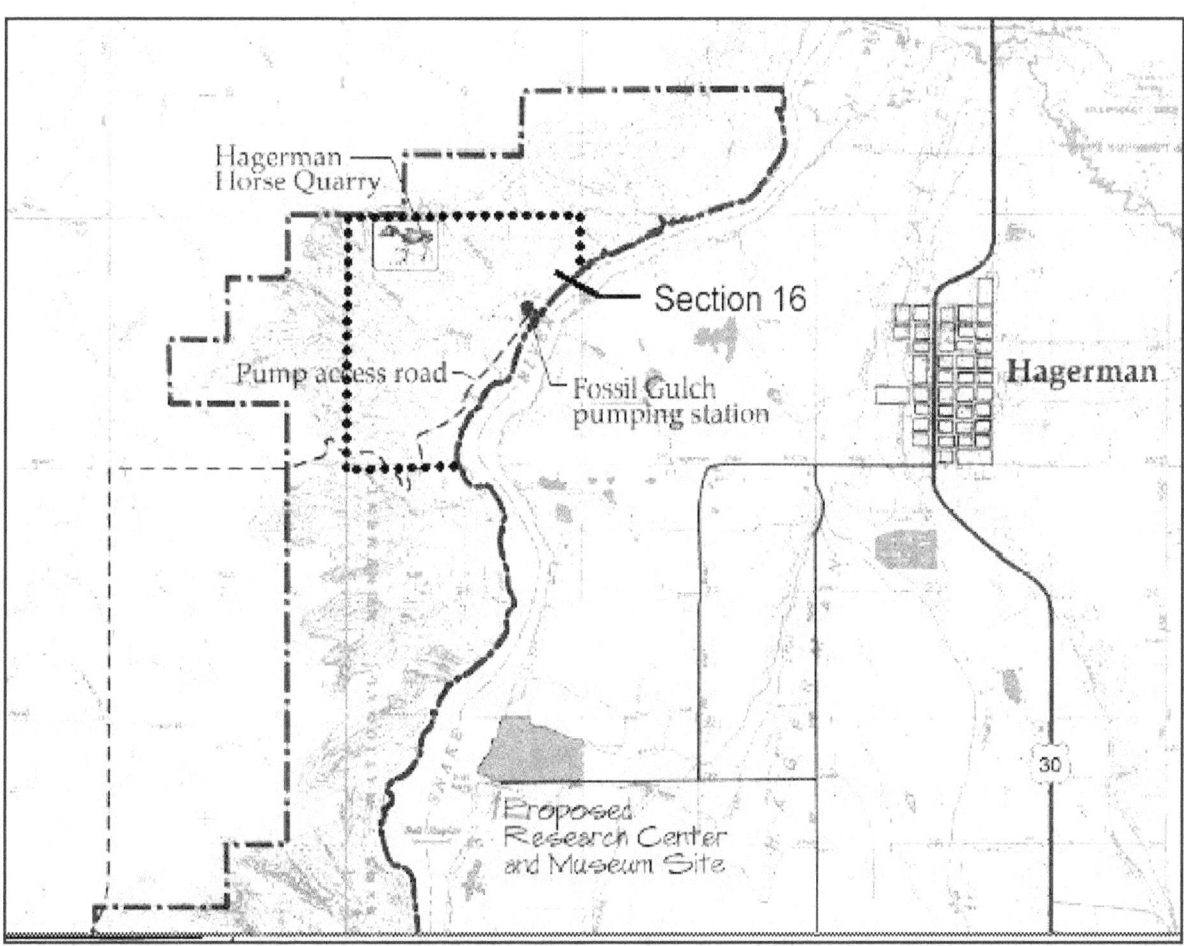

Figure 1. The north section of Hagerman Fossil Beds NM.

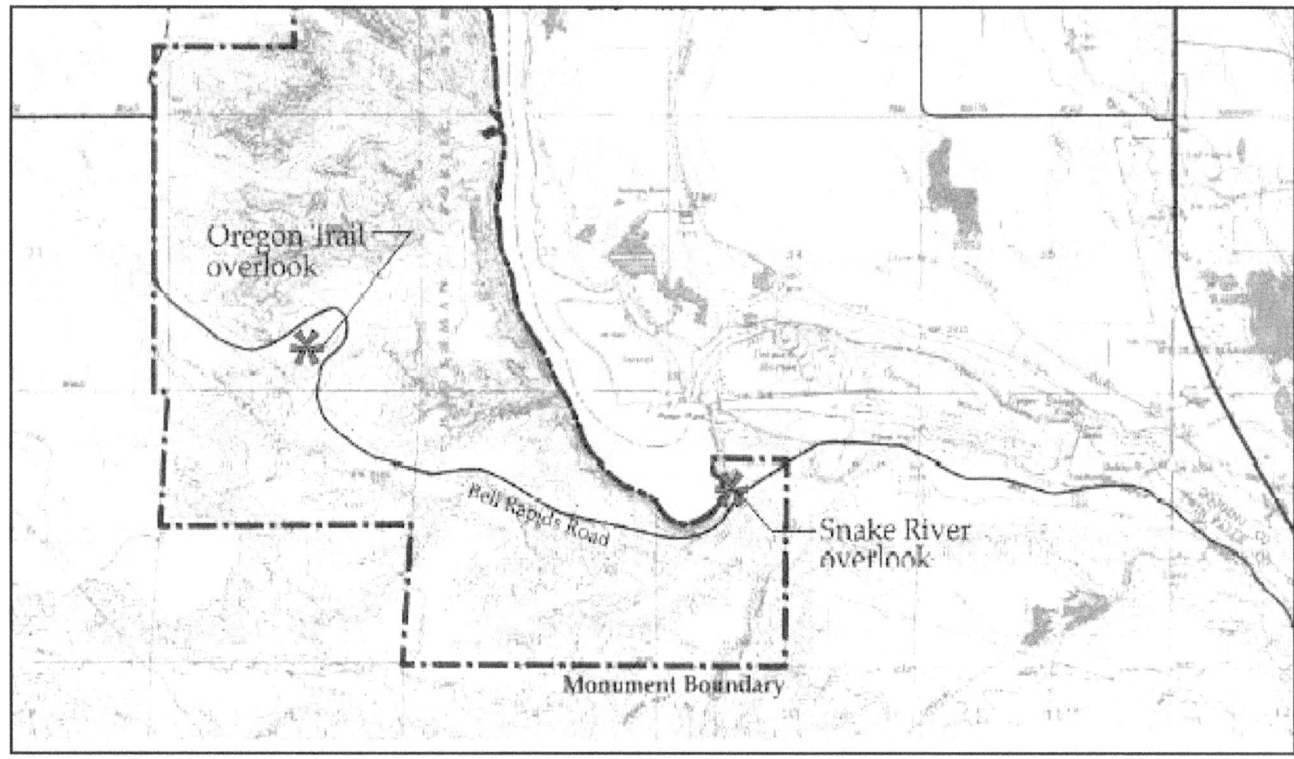

Figure 2. The south section of Hagerman Fossil Beds NM.

The Hagerman Fossil Beds are located along the Snake River and include seven miles of river shoreline. The Thousand Springs natural springs feature is on the east side of the river across from the monument and flows from the basalt cliffs into the river. Elevation of the monument ranges from 3508 ft at the top of the bluff and 2799 ft at the base of the river. The climate in the region is semi-arid, with cool and dry winters and hot and dry summers. Rainfall patterns are variable in the region but most falls in the early spring and late fall. Thirty-year mean annual precipitation available from a weather station 9 miles north of Hagerman in the town of Bliss is 9.5 inches (Western Regional Climate Center 2003). Snowfall represents a small proportion of the winter precipitation but snow pack is ephemeral and rarely lasts more than a few days. Thirty-year January and July mean temperatures from Hagerman are 35 and 67 degrees Fahrenheit, respectively (Western Regional Climate Service 2003). Thirty-year mean January and July minimum and maximum temperatures are 19 and 53 degrees minimum Fahrenheit and 40 and 94 degrees maximum Fahrenheit, respectively (Western Regional Climate Center 2003). It is important to note that winter and summer temperature extremes frequently drop below freezing in the winter and above 100 degrees in the summer.

The Hagerman Valley is located within the Snake River Plain region of the eastern Columbia Plateau. The topography is characterized by large flat plateaus deeply dissected by watercourses. The valley walls rise 600 feet above the Snake River. The sediment layers were deposited when rivers flowing into ancient Lake Idaho flooded the region. The sediments on the bluffs include river sands, thin shale layers deposited in the bonds, clay flood deposits, and occasional volcanic deposits such as ash and basalt. There are many small and ephemeral riparian areas located in the monument. Irrigation water pumped up from the river to agricultural fields on top of the monument has caused seeps to form along the face of the escarpment that has led to large landslides in recent years.

The monument is dominated by sagebrush steppe vegetation but grassland, forest, and riparian areas occur in the monument as well. Common shrubs in the monument include big sagebrush (*Artemisia tridentata*), bitterbrush (*Purshia tridentata*), greasewood (*Sarcobatus vermiculatus*), and rabbitbrush (*Chrysothamnus spp.*). The grasslands consist of oatgrass (*Arrhenatherum elatius*), crested wheatgrass (*Agropyron cristatum*), Great Basin wild rye (*Elymus cinereus*), and bulbous bluegrass (*Poa bulbosa*). Forest habitats consist of black cottonwood (*Populus trichocarpa*) and Russian olive (*Elaeagnus angustifolia*). Riparian vegetation includes black cottonwood, bulrush (*Scirpus spp.*), and cattails (*Typha spp.*).

Non-native vegetation has become established throughout the monument. Some of the dominant non-native species on the monument include Russian olive (*Elaeagnus angustifolia*), Russian thistle (*Salsola kali*), quackgrass (*Agropyron repens*), cheat grass (*Bromus tectorum*), blue mustard (*Chorispora tenella*), tansymustard (*Descurainia sophia*), tumble-mustard (*Sisymbrium altissimum*), and medusa head (*Taeniatherum caput-medusae*). There are dense stands of invasive Russian olive, purple loosestrife (*Lythrum salicaria*), and saltcedar (*Tamarix parviflora*) along the shoreline of the Snake River. Agricultural crops have replaced much of the natural vegetation on private lands adjacent to the monument. The majority of farmlands now consist of a variety of grasses, grains, beets, and potatoes. Small natural fires occur on the monument sporadically. The most recent fire in the monument occurred on the top of Bell Grading near the second scenic overlook in the southern section (Phil Gensler, personal communication). Both fire and the spread of non-native weeds in the monument are strongly influencing the vegetation patterns in the monument and are having an effect on vertebrates in the monument; although this effect has not been quantified in any way.

Methods

The methods utilized in the 2002 inventory generally follow those laid out in the Upper Columbia Basin Network Study Plan (Wright et. al. unpublished) and published literature on inventory methodologies (i.e. Wilson et. al. 1996). Universal Transverse Mercator (UTM) locations given in this report were collected using Garmin 12-channel Etrex hand-held GPS units (Garmin International, Inc, Olathe, KS, USA). Most x and y coordinates (Easting and Northing) are accurate within 10 meters. No accuracy estimate is available for elevation data provided by the GPS unit. The North American Datum of 1927 (NAD 27) was used as the horizontal datum for all locations.

Scientific and common names used in this report follow the Integrated Taxonomic Information System (ITIS). The ITIS follows closely the American Ornithological Union's 7th edition checklist of North American Birds and the USGS Biological Resource Division's unpublished and expanded update of the 1987 Checklist of Vertebrates of the United States, the U.S. Territories, and Canada (ITIS 2003).

The monument boundary was used as the primary boundary of the inventory. However, many species that were observed near the monument were included. This flexibility in boundary was necessary because dispersal abilities of many of the species enable them to move on and off the monument. Because birds are so mobile, we have relied heavily on bird information collected off the monument in the Hagerman Valley. The monument was divided into two sections, a north and south unit as shown in Figures 1 (pg. 3) and 2 (pg. 4).

Expected Species

A variety of methods and materials were used to determine which species of birds, mammals, and herpetofauna were expected to occur in the monument. Expert opinion was used to critically examine published range maps and distribution literature from a variety of sources, historic park service reports, and observations. Habitat types occurring in and adjacent to the monument were also carefully considered. Range, elevation, habitat, and species detectability were considered and developed into a criteria set that was used to place species into "expected" and "possible but not expected" categories. Detectability was included in the consideration in order to address species that naturally occur in low abundances or are in some other way very difficult to confirm through established survey protocols. Species such as the Merriam's shrew (*Sorex merriami*) often require years of consistent trapping to document and these species were considered as "possible but not expected" in this inventory (Kirkland et. al. 1997, Verts and Carraway 1998). Species that met all four criteria were included as "expected".

Published and unpublished sources used to determine the range, habitat, and elevation requirements of birds, mammals, and herpetofauna included the Peterson Field Guide to Western Birds (Peterson 1990), National Audubon Society Sibley Guide to the Birds (Sibley 2000), National Audubon Society Field Guide to North American Mammals (Whitaker 1996), Digital Atlas of Idaho (2003), Land Mammals of Oregon (Verts and Carraway 1998), The Mammals of Idaho (Larrison 1981), Ground-Dwelling Squirrels of the Pacific Northwest (Yensen and Sherman 2003), Reptiles of the Northwest (St. John 2002), Amphibians & Reptiles of the Pacific Northwest (Nussbaum et. al. 1983), Idaho Species of Special Concern Element State Ranking

Review (Engle and Harris 2001), and Idaho's Amphibian & Reptiles (Nongame Wildlife Leaflet #7, Idaho Fish & Game). Information provided by Sarah Harris of the College of Southern Idaho, Kent Fothergill of the Twin Falls Audubon Society, and the Thousand Springs Nature Conservancy Reserve were also used to develop an expected bird list.

Sampling Site Selection

A stratified random sampling design was used to locate mammal and herpetofauna trap locations in the monument. The monument was stratified by habitat, slope, and aspect. Four habitat categories were used and included shrub, grassland, forest, and riparian. Two aspect categories were used and included southwest and northeast. Three slope categories included 0 degrees, 0-5 degrees, and 5-20 degrees. In order to ensure dispersion, the monument was divided in half and an equal number of points were allocated to each half. A random selection of points were generated and were included if they landed within one of the aspect and slope categories, and an equal number were allocated to each habitat type. Points within 50 meters of the road were not included, but points that were near trailheads and roads were preferred in order to reduce travel time between sample points. A total of 12 points were located in the southern portion of the monument and 16 were located in the northern portion. Because of the small amount of riparian area in the monument, fewer points were located in that habitat type than in the other three.

A subjective, non-random sampling site selection procedure was used for visual encounter surveys and for some small mammal trapping. This approach was determined to be the most efficient and effective given the primary objective of the inventory and the limited number of field personnel. Specific habitats and locations were identified and targeted for sampling in order to maximize the opportunities to encounter as many previously undocumented species as possible. While a majority of the inventory effort was concentrated near roads and trails due to logistical considerations, effort was made to periodically search more remote portions of the monument in order to ensure adequate dispersion of sampling locations. Seasonal changes in species presence or detectability were also an issue and required multiple visits to sites over the course of the year. Data from Christmas Bird Counts in the Hagerman Valley were included, which were conducted by following pre-established non-randomly selected routes in the area.

Visual Encounter Surveys

The visual encounter survey was one of the primary methods used to inventory birds, mammals, and herpetofauna during the 2003 field season. Visual encounter surveys were conducted by methodically searching target habitats. Cover turning was incorporated into the herpetological surveys. Weather was a significant factor in the herpetological surveys, and surveys were normally conducted during times and days when temperature, wind, and precipitation were optimal for reptile and amphibian activity. Incidental observations made of all vertebrates in or near the monument during travel and other inventory activities were included under the visual encounter category as well. Incidental observations contributed significantly to the overall success of the 2003 inventory and enabled participation from volunteers and NPS staff. Visual encounter data for birds collected between 1992-1998 in the Thousand Springs Nature Conservancy Reserve were included in the inventory. Visual encounter data collected during the annual Hagerman Valley Christmas Bird Count from 1974-2003 were included. Bird observations made by Kent Fothergill of the Twin Falls Audubon Society, between 1999-2003 in and adjacent to the monument were also included. Ancillary information recorded during visual encounter surveys included age, sex, time, location, habitat, and notes of interest.

Trapping

A variety of trapping techniques were used to inventory small mammals and herpetofauna and generally followed procedures outlined in Jones et. al. (1996), Cooperrider et. al. (1986), and the Upper Columbia Basin Network Study Plan. Capture and handling procedures were consistent with those outlined by the Ad Hoc Committee on Acceptable Field Methods in Mammalogy (1987) and the University of Idaho Institutional Animal Care and Use Committee.

Small Mammals

The primary technique used for small mammals involved the use of Sherman live traps placed along 50-meter transects. Trap stations were established approximately every 5 meters and 1 live trap was placed at each station. Transects were pre-baited for 1 day and traps were set for two to four consecutive nights. Traps were placed non-randomly near microhabitat features and mammal sign in order to maximize capture success. Traps were baited with peanut butter, crimped oats, and black oil sunflower seeds. Liver and raw chicken was used to target shrews.

Miscellaneous trapping techniques included the use of Havahart and Tomahawk wire cage traps targeted for skunks, weasels, and muskrats. Auxiliary data related with small mammal captures included time, date, location, weather, moon phase, topography, age, sex, and habitat.

Amphibians and Reptiles

Funnel traps were the primary trapping technique used to capture herpetofauna. Funnel trap locations were chosen based on a stratified random sample. Funnel traps were located in 28 sampling locations in the monument. Three funnel traps were located at each site and placed at the end of 7-meter drift fence arms. These traps were effective at capturing small mammals as well.

Pitfall trap arrays were another effective method used to capture reptiles and amphibians. Pitfall arrays were placed on southwest facing slopes in shrub habitat at randomly chosen locations established for funnel traps. Two pitfall arrays were placed in the north section and two arrays were placed in the southern section. Pitfalls were constructed from #10 size coffee cans and 7-meter strips of aluminum and tin metal flashing used as drift fencing in an "X" formation.

Road Surveys

Road surveys were conducted in the reptile and amphibian inventory. The small number of roads in the monument limited the overall usage of this technique, although it did lead to the documentation of several important species of herpetofauna. Road surveys for reptiles and amphibians were conducted in the evening and night hours during warm weather and lasted for several hours or until temperatures had cooled below the point at which reptile and amphibian activity could be expected. Road surveys also factor heavily into the Hagerman Valley Christmas Bird Counts and the results of those are also included in the inventory.

Species Documentation Methods

Species encountered during the inventory were documented using photography, voucher specimens from incidental mortality, and field observation records. Mammal specimens not kept by the monument are permanently housed at the University of Washington Burke Museum of Natural History in Seattle, Washington. Herpetofauna specimens are permanently housed at the Idaho State University Museum of Natural History. In addition to specimens and photographs, data sheets and field notes were kept on all inventory activities and species encountered. Photocopies have been made of all data sheets and field notes and are permanently housed with the Upper Columbia Basin Network in Moscow, ID.

Results

Historic Information

No comprehensive vertebrate inventory has been conducted in the monument prior to the current I & M project. Little historic vertebrate information is available from the monument. In 1995, the Idaho Power sponsored a survey of plants and animals as part of a FERC relicensing study conducted along the Snake River (Holthuijzen 1995a, 1995b, 1995c). The results of this report were used to provide documentation of bird and mammal species present in or near the monument. A modest effort was made to document birds and mammals as part of a review of exotic plant pests in the monument in 1998 and those results are also used as species documentation (Monello and Wright 1998). A number of vertebrate sightings made be monument staff were used as historical evidence of species presence.

Birds

Expected and Confirmed Species

A total of 154 birds are expected to occur in or near the monument and 153 (99%) species have been confirmed. Forty-one unexpected species have also been confirmed, bringing the total number of birds confirmed in or near the monument to 194. Table 1 (pg. 21) lists the expected and unexpected species and their confirmation status.

Mammals

Expected and Confirmed Species

A total of 33 species of mammals (excluding bats) are expected to occur in or adjacent to the monument. Twenty-six species were documented in 2002, one of which, the white-tailed antelope ground squirrel (*Ammospermophilus leucurus*), was not expected to occur in the park. Seventy-nine percent of the expected species have been documented. The list of expected and possible species and their current status in the monument is shown in Table 2 (pg. 26).

Mammal Trapping

Trapping effort for small and medium sized non-volant mammals with Sherman and Havahart live traps totaled 898 trap nights. Mammals caught in funnel traps and pitfall arrays used for herpetofauna were included in capture results but not in the trap night calculation. Total capture of non-volant mammals was 251 individuals. Deer mice (*Peromyscus maniculatus*) were the most abundant mammals captured, representing 82% of all captures. The harvest mouse (*Reithrodontomys megalotis*) was the second most abundant mammal captured, representing 8% of all captures. Table 3 (pg. 28) shows the location and trapping effort information and Table 4 (pg. 30) shows the results from the 2003 mammal trapping effort. Figures 3 (pg. 17) and 4 (pg. 18) show the location of mammal transects and Figures 5 (pg. 19) and 6 (pg. 20) show the locations of funnel traps and pitfall arrays.

Amphibians and Reptiles

Expected and Confirmed Species
A total of 18 species of herpetofauna are expected to occur in and adjacent to the Hagerman Fossil Beds National Monument. The 2003 inventory confirmed 14 of those species (78%). Ten of those species were reptiles and the other four were amphibians. Table 5 (pg. 33) shows the list of expected species and unexpected species and their status on the monument. Table 6 (pg.34) lists the location and habitat information for the funnel traps and pitfall arrays. Table 7 (pg.35) shows the capture results for herpetofauna captured during the inventory. Figures 5 (pg. 19) and 6 (pg. 20) show the location of the pitfall arrays and funnel traps.

Discussion

Birds

Hagerman Fossil Beds National Monument and the area surrounding the monument in the Hagerman Valley host a rich diversity of bird life. The Snake River and adjacent wetlands such as the Thousand Springs Reserve provide valuable resources for migrating and over-wintering waterfowl and wading species. The upland sagebrush steppe and grasslands provide important habitat for unique species of sparrows such as the Brewer's sparrow (*Spizella breweri*) and grasshopper sparrow (*Ammodramus savannarum*). A surprising diversity of insectivorous flycatchers (*Empidonax spp.*) have been documented in the monument, some of which may be breeding in the monument. Of particular interest is the willow flycatcher (*Empidonax trailii*), which is in decline in many parts of its range.

Mammals

The 2003 mammal inventory began with very little historic information. The white-tailed antelope ground squirrel was located twice on the monument in different locations. This species was not expected to occur in the monument and represents a modest eastward range extension approximately 40 miles (Yensen and Sherman 2003).

Shrews were a group of interest for the 2003 mammal inventory. The vagrant shrew (*Sorex vagrans*) is expected to occur in wetter portions of the monument. The Merriam's shrew (*Sorex merrriami*) may occur in the monument but the species is notoriously hard to capture and its habitat requirements are poorly known, making it difficult to effectively target this species (Kirkland et. al. 1997, Verts and Carraway 1998). Shrews in general are a poorly known group in Idaho and any future information collected on the family in HAFO will make a significant contribution to the understanding of their ecology and conservation (Digital Atlas of Idaho 2003).

Two species of voles were not found on the monument during the inventory. The long-tailed vole (*Microtus longicaudus*) and the sagebrush vole (*Lemmiscus curtatus*) are uncommon and can be difficult to capture. Their absence in 2003 capture results may suggest that the monument was experiencing a low point in the microtine population cycle. The sagebrush vole was captured in the monument during the Idaho Power study conducted in 1995.

Several carnivores, the long-tailed weasel (*Mustela frenata*), mink (*Mustela frenata*), spotted skunk (*Spilogale gracilis*), river otter (*Lutra canadensis*), and the bobcat (*Lynx rufus*) are also expected to occur in the monument but are difficult to document. These species, especially the last three, are probably most likely to be documented by monument staff or visitors during chance encounters in the field. Staff should be alerted of the need for these species' documentation.

Finally, the pronghorn (*Antilocapra americana*) was confirmed in one location during the inventory. This species was found outside of the monument boundaries in the alfalfa field above the bluffs in the north section. The fields near the monument provide an excellent food source for many animals in the area.

Amphibians and Reptiles

Fourteen reptile and amphibian species were found during the 2003 inventory and four species of reptiles that were expected to occur were not found. Undocumented species include the long-toed salamander (*Ambystoma macrodactylum*), northern leopard frog (*Rana pipiens*), longnose leopard lizard (*Gambelis wislizenii*), and the western skink (*Eumeces skiltonianus*).

The Pacific tree frog was confirmed in this study based only on the calls that were heard at dusk. This species occurred in the cottonwood and Russian olive groves along the river.

The Sagebrush Lizard (*Sceloporus graciosus*) was found in one location in the monument. This species was found on the north end near north pitfall 1. University of Idaho biologists also encountered this species during a birding outing in the monument during 2001.

The long-toed salamander likely occurs in the monument and may be encountered in the future by looking under logs in moist woodlands in the monument and around the paleontology buildings and riparian area on the east side of the river.

The northern leopard frog has been documented near the Hagerman Valley in the past and is expected to occur there (Digital Atlas of Idaho 2003). However, this species is experiencing dramatic declines in distribution in the Pacific Northwest due to disease and competition from exotic species such as the bullfrog (*Rana catesbiana*) (Corkran and Thoms 1996).

The longnose leopard lizard is expected to occur in the monument but invasion of cheatgrass and other annual grasses may be reducing the habitat quality of the monument for this species (St. John 2002). This species depends on open tracts of loose soils in shrub steppe for foraging and the species has been lost from many areas where invasive vegetation has closed in (St. John 2002, Peterson personal communication).

Literature Cited

Ad hoc Committee on Acceptable Field Methods in Mammalogy. 1987. Acceptable field methods in mammalogy: preliminary guidelines approved by the American Society of Mammalogists. Journal of Mammalogy 68(4) supplement.

Cooperrider, A.Y., R.J. Boyd, and H.R. Stuart. 1986. Inventory and monitoring of wildlife habitat. U.S. Dept. of Interior Bureau of Land Management Service Center. Denver, CO.

Corkran, C. C. and C.R. Thoms. 1996. Amphibians of Oregon, Washington, and British Columbia. Lone Pine Publishing, Renton, WA.

Digital Atlas of Idaho. 2003. Digital atlas of Idaho: Idaho's natural history online. Idaho Museum of Natural History. Idaho State University, Pocatello, Idaho. http://imnh.isu.edu/digitalatlas (retrieved 2003)

Engle, J. C. and C. E. Harris. 2001. Idaho species of special concern element state ranking review. Nongame and Endangered Wildlife Program Conservation Data Center. Idaho Department of Fish and Game.

Holthuijzen, Anthonie, M.A. 1995a. An investigation of small mammals in the Hagerman Study Area. Technical Report E32-H, Idaho Power FERC Relicensing Report.

Holthuijzen, Anthonie, M.A. 1995b. An investigation of the herptile community in the Hagerman Study Area. Technical Report E32-2, Idaho Power FERC Relicensing Report.

Holthuijzen, Anthonie, M.A. 1995b. Holthuijzen, Anthonie, M.A. 1995b. 1995c. An investigation of nongame birds in the Hagerman Study Area. Technical Report E32-M, Idaho Power FERC Relicensing Report.

Idaho Fish and Game. 1994. Idaho's amphibian and reptiles, Nongame Wildlife leaflet #7.

ITIS. 2003. Integrated taxonomic information system on-line database system. U.S. Department of Agriculture. http://www.itis.usda.gov (retrieved 1/10/03).

Jones, C., W.J. McSea, M.J. Conroy, and T.H. Kunz. 1996. Capturing mammals. In D.E. Wilson, F.R. Cole, J.D. Nichols, R. Rudran, and M.S. Foster (eds.) Measuring and monitoring biological diversity: standard methods for mammals. Smithsonian Institution Press, Washington D.C.

Kirkland, G.L. Jr., R.R. Parmenter, and R.E. Skoog. 1997. A five-species assemblage of shrews from the sagebrush-steppe of Wyoming. Journal of Mammalogy 78(1):83-89.

Larrison, E.J. 1981. Mammals of Idaho. University Press of Idaho, Moscow, ID.

Monello, R.J. and G.R. Wright. 1998. Exotic pest plan inventory, mapping, and priorities for control in parks in the Pacific Northwest, and initial bird and small mammal survey results for parks in the Pacific Northwest. USGS Idaho Cooperative Fish and Wildlife Research Unit, University of Idaho, Moscow, ID.

Nussbaum, R. A., E.D. Broodie, and R. M. Storm. 1983. Amphibian and reptiles of the Pacific Northwest. University of Idaho Press.

Peterson, R.T. 1990. A field guide to western birds. The Peterson Field Guide Series. Houghton Mifflin Co., Boston.

Rachlow, J. and L. Svancara. 2003. Pygmy rabbit habitat in Idaho. University of Idaho Fish and Wildlife Resources and Landscapes Dynamics Lab, Moscow, ID.

Sibley, D.A. 2000. The Sibley guide to the birds. National Audubon Society. Chanticleer Press, New York, NY.

St. John, A. D. 2002. Reptiles of the northwest: Alaska to California, rockies to the coast. Lone Pine Publishing, Renton, WA.

Stokes, D., C. Rochester, R. Fisher, and T. Case. 2001. Herpetological monitoring using pitfall trapping design in southern California. U.S. Geological Survey (open file report). Biological Resources Division. San Diego, CA.

Verts, B.J. and L.N. Carraway. 1998. Land mammals of Oregon. University of California Press, Berkeley, CA.

Western Regional Climate Center. 2003. Idaho Climate Summaries. Desert Research Institute, Reno, NV. www.wrcc.dri.edu/summary/climsmid.html (accessed 2003).

Whitaker, J.O., Jr. 1996. National Audubon Society Field Guide to North American Mammals. Alfred A. Knopf Inc., New York, NY.

Wilson, D.E., F.R. Cole, J.D. Nichols, R. Rudran, and M.S. Foster. 1996. Measuring and monitoring biological diversity: Standard methods for mammals. Smithsonian Institution Press, Washington, D.C.

Wright, G.R., L. Garrett, and D. Foster. Unpublished. A study plan to inventory vascular plants and vertebrates in national park service units in the Upper Columbia Basin Network. University of Idaho Department of Fish and Wildlife. Moscow, ID.

Yensen, E. and P.W. Sherman. 2003. Ground dwelling squirrels of the Pacific Northwest. U.S. Fish and Wildlife Service, Snake River Fish and Wildlife Office, Boise, ID.

Appendix A. Figures and Tables

Figures

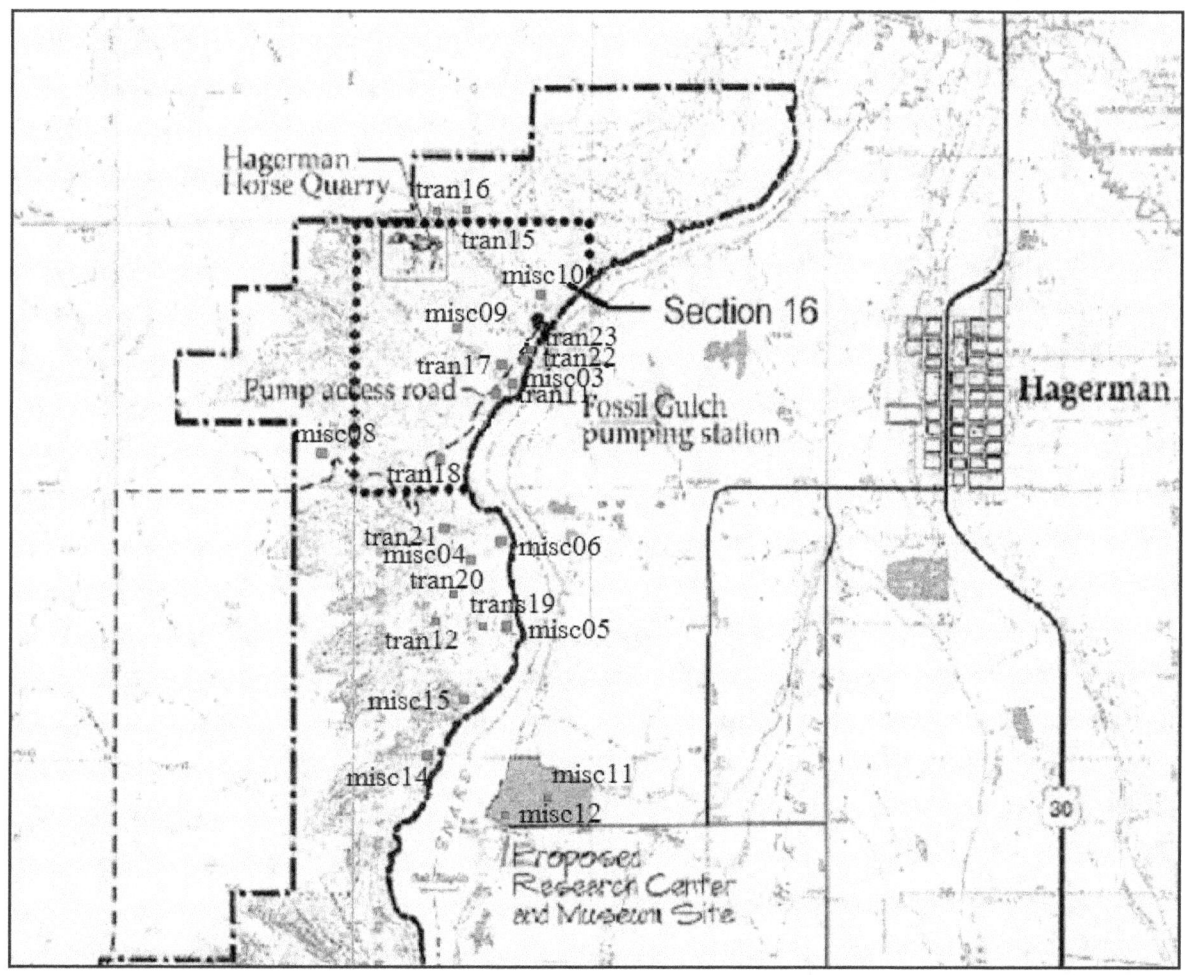

Figure 3. Mammal transect locations in the north section of Hagerman Fossil Beds NM during the 2003 inventory.

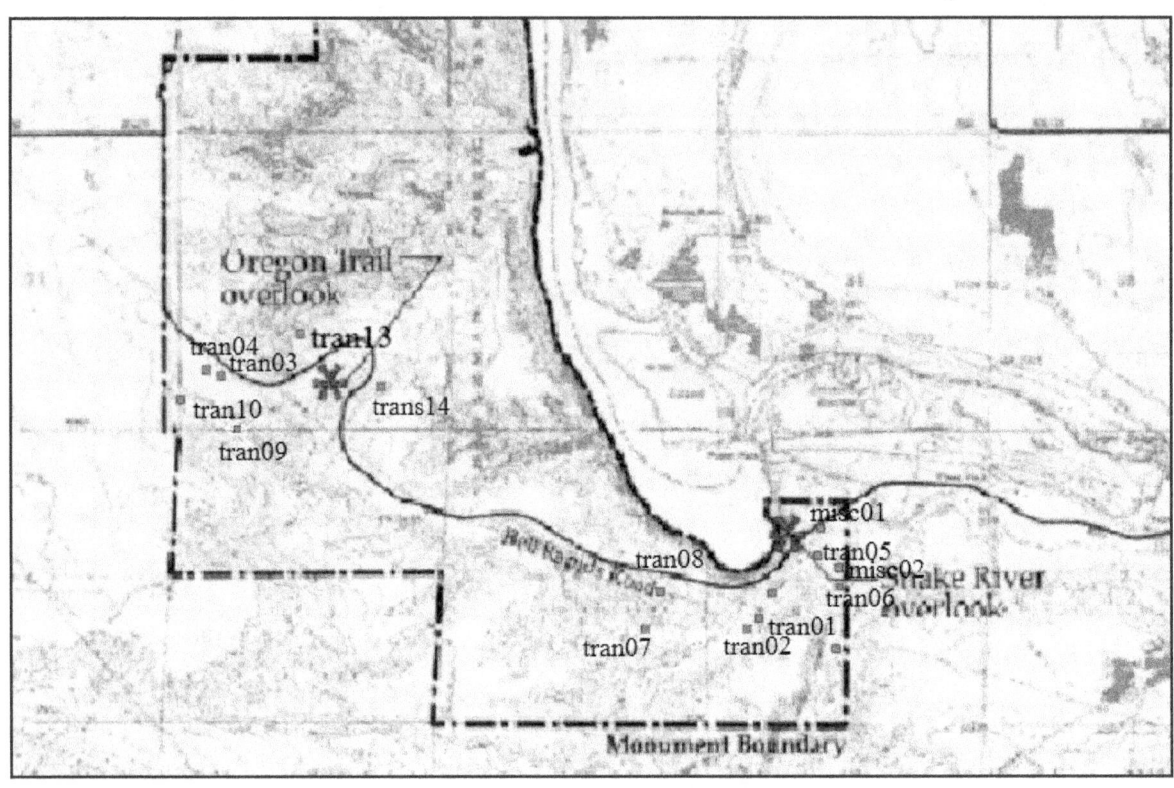

Figure 4. Mammal transect locations in the south section of Hagerman Fossil Beds NM during the 2003 inventory.

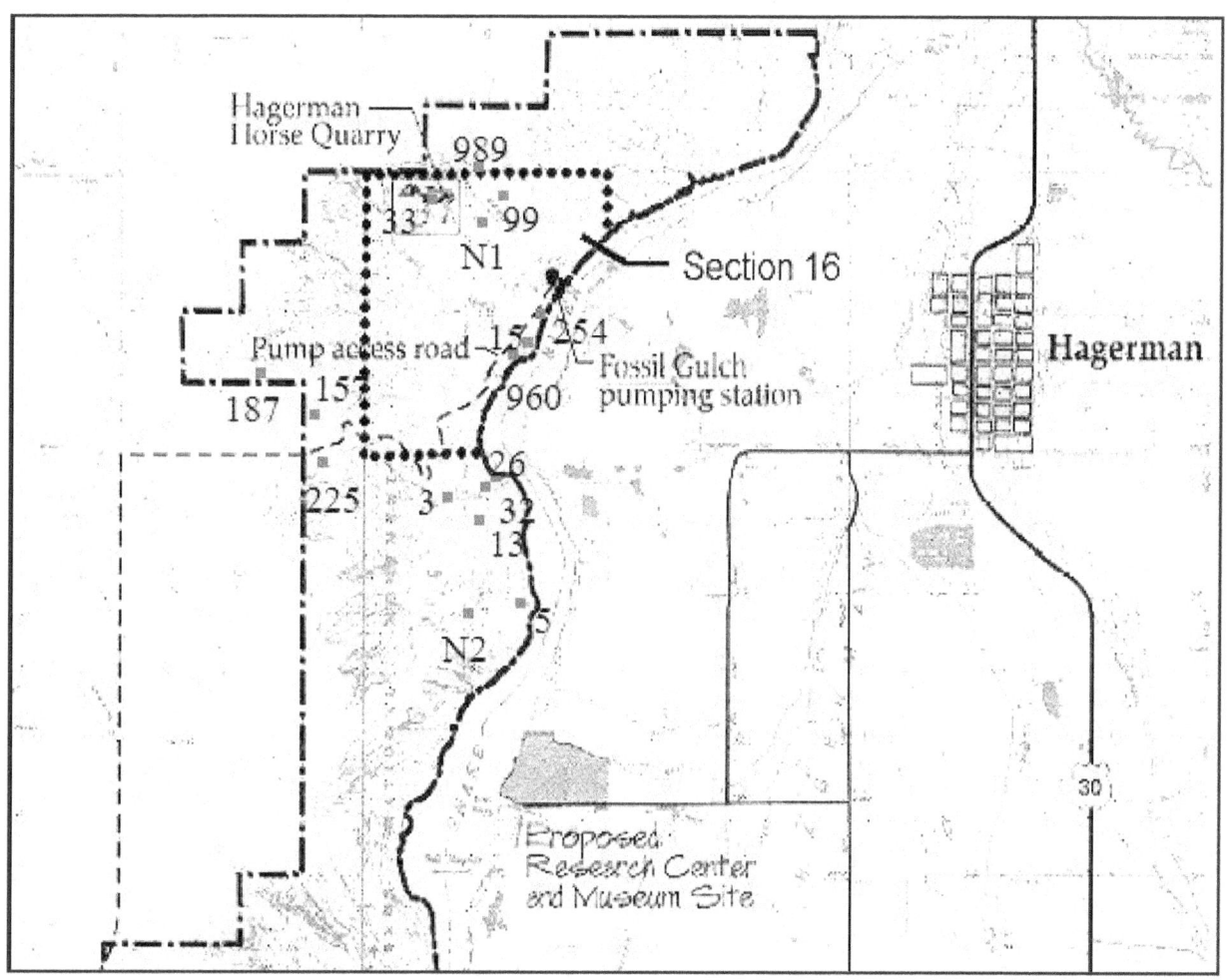

Figure 5. Funnel trap and pitfall locations in the north section of Hagerman Fossil Beds NM during the 2003 inventory.

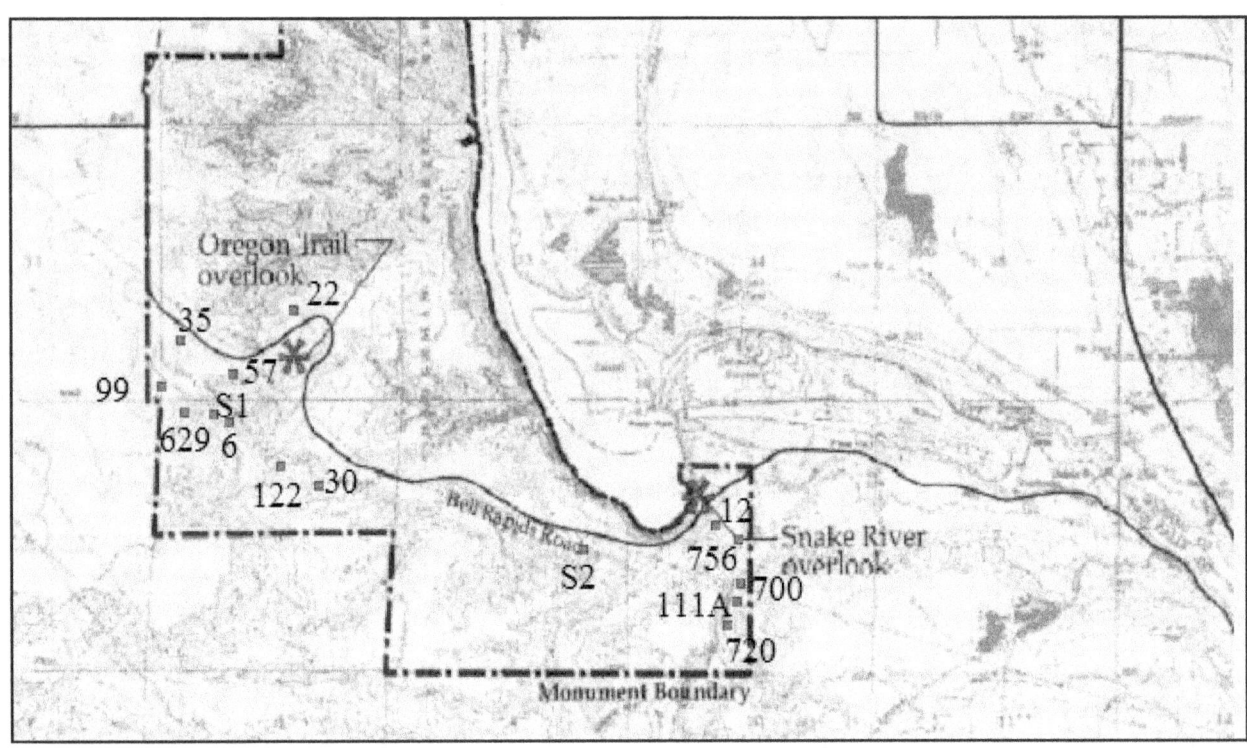

Figure 6. Funnel traps and pitfall arrays in the south section of Hagerman Fossil Beds NM during the 2003 inventory.

Tables

Table 1. List of expected and possible bird species and their confirmation status in or near Hagerman Fossil Beds NM.

Common Name	Expected	Confirmed	A	B	C	D	E	F
Common Loon	1	1	1	1	1			
Pied-billed Grebe	1	1	1	1	1		1	
Eared Grebe	1	1	1	1	1			
Western Grebe	1	1	1	1	1		1	
Clark's Grebe	1	1		1	1	1	1	
American White Pelican	1	1	1	1	1	1	1	1
Double-crested Cormorant	1	1	1	1	1	1	1	
Great Blue Heron	1	1	1	1	1		1	
Great Egret	1	1	1	1	1			
Snowy Egret		1	1	1				
Cattle Egret		1		1	1			
Black-crowned Night Heron	1	1	1	1	1			
White-faced Ibis			1					
Turkey Vulture	1	1	1		1			1
Snow Goose	1	1	1	1				
Canada Goose	1	1	1	1	1	1	1	
Tundra Swan	1	1	1	1	1			
Wood Duck	1	1		1	1			
Gadwall	1	1	1	1	1		1	
American Wigeon	1	1	1	1	1		1	
European Wigeon		1	1					
Mallard	1	1	1	1	1	1	1	1
Blue-winged Teal	1	1	1	1	1			
Cinnamon Teal	1	1	1	1	1		1	
Northern Shoveler	1	1	1	1	1			1
Northern Pintail	1	1	1	1	1			
Green-winged Teal	1	1	1	1	1			
Canvasback	1	1		1	1			
Redhead	1	1	1	1	1	1	1	
Ring-necked Duck	1	1	1	1	1		1	
Tufted Duck		1			1			
Greater Scaup		1		1	1			
Lesser Scaup	1	1	1	1	1		1	
Long-tailed Duck		1			1			
Bufflehead	1	1	1	1	1		1	
Barrow's Goldeneye		1		1	1			
Common Goldeneye	1	1	1	1	1	1	1	
Hooded Merganser	1	1	1	1	1			
Common Merganser	1	1	1	1	1			
Ruddy Duck	1	1	1	1	1			

Table 1. List of expected and possible bird species and their confirmation status in or near Hagerman Fossil Beds NM (continued).

Common Name	Expected	Confirmed	Sources[a]					
			A	B	C	D	E	F
Osprey	1	1			1	1	1	
Bald Eagle	1	1	1	1	1			
Northern Harrier	1	1	1	1	1	1	1	1
Sharp-shinned Hawk	1	1	1	1	1			
Cooper's Hawk	1	1		1	1			
Northern Goshawk		1		1	1			
Swainson's Hawk	1							
Red-tailed Hawk	1	1	1	1	1	1	1	1
Ferruginous Hawk	1	1			1			
Rough-legged Hawk	1	1		1	1			
Golden Eagle	1	1	1	1	1			
American Kestrel	1	1	1	1	1		1	1
Merlin	1	1			1			
Peregrine Falcon	1	1		1	1			
Prairie Falcon	1	1			1			
Gray Partridge	1	1	1	1	1			
Chukar	1	1			1			1
Ring-necked Pheasant	1	1	1	1	1	1	1	1
Sage Grouse								
California Quail	1	1	1	1	1	1	1	1
Virginia Rail	1	1		1	1		1	1
Sora Rail	1	1	1	1	1		1	
American Coot	1	1	1	1	1	1	1	
Sandhill Crane								
Black-bellied Plover				1				
Semi-palmated Plover				1				
Killdeer	1	1	1	1	1	1	1	
Black-necked Stilt				1				
American Avocet	1	1	1	1				
Greater Yellowlegs				1				
Lesser Yellowlegs				1				
Willet				1				
Spotted Sandpiper	1	1	1	1				
Long-billed Curlew	1	1		1				
Marbled Godwit		1		1				
Sanderling		1		1				
Semi-palmated Sandpiper		1		1				
Least Sandpiper		1		1				
Long-billed Dowitcher		1	1	1				
Short-billed Dowitcher		1	1					
Common Snipe	1	1			1	1	1	
Wilson's Phalarope	1	1				1		

Table 1. List of expected and possible bird species and their confirmation status in or near Hagerman Fossil Beds NM (continued).

Common Name	Expected	Confirmed	Sources[a]					
			A	B	C	D	E	F
Franklin's Gull	1	1			1		1	
Ring-billed Gull	1	1	1	1	1		1	
California Gull	1	1	1	1	1			
Herring Gull	1	1		1	1			
Caspian Tern	1	1	1	1				
Forster's Tern	1	1	1	1			1	
Black Tern								
Rock Dove	1	1		1	1	1	1	
Mourning Dove	1	1	1	1	1	1	1	1
Barn Owl	1	1	1	1	1			
Western Screech Owl	1	1	1	1	1			
Great Horned Owl	1	1	1	1	1		1	1
Burrowing Owl	1	1					1	
Long-eared Owl	1	1	1		1		1	
Short-eared Owl	1	1	1	1	1			
Northern Saw-whet Owl		1		1				
Common Nighthawk	1	1	1	1				
Common Poorwill	1	1					1	
White-throated Swift		1		1				
Black-chinned Hummingbird	1	1		1				
Calliope Hummingbird								
Broad-tailed Hummingbird		1		1				
Rufous Hummingbird		1		1				
Belted Kingfisher	1	1	1	1	1			1
Downy Woodpecker	1	1		1	1			1
Hairy Woodpecker	1							
Northern Flicker	1	1	1	1	1			
Western Wood-Pewee	1							
Willow Flycatcher		1		1				
Dusky Flycatcher	1	1	1					
Gray Flycatcher	1	1					1	
Ash-throated Flycatcher	1	1		1				
Hammond's Flycatcher		1					1	
Cordilleran Flycatcher		1					1	
Say's Phoebe	1	1		1				
Western Kingbird	1	1	1	1				
Eastern Kingbird	1	1	1	1				
Northern Shrike	1	1		1	1			
Loggerhead Shrike	1	1		1	1			1
Warbling Vireo	1							
Red-eyed Vireo		1	1					
Steller's Jay		1			1			

Table 1. List of expected and possible bird species and their confirmation status in or near Hagerman Fossil Beds NM (continued).

Common Name	Expected	Confirmed	Sources[a]					
			A	B	C	D	E	F
Blue Jay		1			1			
Western Scrub Jay		1			1			
Black-billed Magpie	1	1	1	1	1	1	1	1
American Crow	1	1	1	1	1	1	1	
Common Raven	1	1	1	1	1		1	
Horned Lark	1	1		1	1		1	1
Tree Swallow	1							
Violet-green Swallow	1	1	1	1				1
Northern Rough-winged Swallow	1	1	1	1	1	1	1	
Bank Swallow	1	1	1			1	1	
Cliff Swallow	1	1	1	1			1	
Barn Swallow	1	1	1	1				
Black-capped Chickadee	1	1		1	1			
Mountain Chickadee	1	1	1	1	1			
Bushtit	1	1			1			
Red-breasted Nuthatch	1	1		1	1			
White-breasted Nuthatch		1			1			
Brown Creeper	1	1		1	1			
Rock Wren	1	1	1	1	1			
Canyon Wren	1	1		1	1		1	
Marsh Wren	1	1	1	1	1		1	
House Wren	1	1		1	1			
Winter Wren		1		1	1			
American Dipper	1	1	1	1	1			
Golden Crowned Kinglet	1	1		1	1			
Ruby crowned Kinglet	1	1	1	1	1		1	1
Mountain Bluebird	1	1			1			
Townsend's Solitaire	1	1		1	1		1	1
Swainson's Thrush								
Hermit Thrush		1		1	1			
Varied Thrush		1		1	1			
American Robin	1	1	1	1	1	1	1	1
Gray Catbird								
Northern Mockingbird								
Sage Thrasher	1	1		1			1	
European Starling	1	1	1	1	1	1	1	
American Pipit	1	1		1	1			
Bohemian Waxwing		1			1			
Cedar Waxwing	1	1		1	1			
Orange-crowned Warbler	1	1			1			
Yellow-rumped Warbler	1	1	1	1	1			

Table 1. List of expected and possible bird species and their confirmation status in or near Hagerman Fossil Beds NM (continued).

Common Name	Expected	Confirmed	Sources[a] A	B	C	D	E	F
Yellow Warbler	1	1	1	1				
Common Yellowthroat				1				
Wilson's Warbler	1	1		1				
Yellow-breasted Chat	1	1		1		1		
Western Tanager	1	1	1	1				
Green-tailed Towhee	1							
Spotted Towhee	1	1	1	1	1			
American Tree Sparrow	1	1		1	1			
Chipping Sparrow	1	1	1	1			1	
Brewer's Sparrow	1	1						1
Vesper Sparrow	1	1		1			1	
Lark Sparrow	1	1	1	1				
Sage Sparrow	1	1					1	
Savannah Sparrow	1	1						1
Grasshopper Sparrow		1					1	
Fox Sparrow	1	1		1	1	1		
Song Sparrow	1	1	1	1	1	1	1	1
Lincoln's Sparrow	1	1		1	1			
White-crowned Sparrow	1	1	1	1	1		1	1
Harris Sparrow		1		1	1			
Dark-eyed Junco	1	1	1	1	1		1	
Snow Bunting		1			1			
Black-headed Grosbeak	1	1		1				
Lazuli Bunting	1	1		1		1		
Bobolink								
Red-winged Blackbird	1	1	1	1	1	1	1	1
Western Meadowlark	1	1	1	1	1	1	1	1
Yellow-headed Blackbird	1	1	1	1	1			
Brewer's Blackbird	1	1	1	1	1		1	
Brown-headed Cowbird	1	1	1	1				
Northern Oriole	1	1	1	1	1		1	
Cassin's Finch	1	1			1			
House Finch	1	1		1	1			
Pine Siskin	1	1		1	1			
American Goldfinch	1	1	1	1	1	1		
Evening Grosbeak	1	1			1			
House Sparrow	1	1		1	1			
Total	**153**	**180**						
Total Percent Confirmed		**0.96**						

[a] A= Idaho Power Study, B= Thousand Springs Nature Conservancy Reserve Bird List 1992-1998, C= Hagerman Valley Christmas Bird Counts (1976-2004), D= Monello and Wright 1998, E= 2001 University of Idaho Fieldwork, F=2003 University of Idaho Fieldwork

Table 2. List of mammal species expected or possible in the monument and their status during the 2003 inventory.

Common Name	Scientific Name	Expected	Confirmed
Vagrant Shrew	*Sorex vagrans*	1	0
Merriam's Shrew	*Sorex merriami*	0	0
Little Brown Myotis	*Myotis lucifugus*	1	0
Yuma Myotis	*Myotis yumanensis*	1	0
Western Pipistrelle	*Pipistrellus hesperus*	1	0
Big Brown Bat	*Eptesicus fuscus*	1	0
Spotted Bat	*Euderma maculatum*	0	0
Townsend's Big-eared Bat	*Corynorhinus townsendii*	0	0
Pallid Bat	*Antrozous pallidus*	1	0
Western Small-footed Myotis	*Myotis ciliolabrum*	1	0
California Myotis	*Myotis californicus*	0	0
Fringed Myotis	*Myotis thysanodes*	0	0
Long-eared Myotis	*Myotis evotis*	0	0
Long-legged Myotis	*Myotis volans*	0	0
Silver-haired Bat	*Lasionycteris noctivagans*	0	0
Hoary Bat	*Lasiurus cinereus*	0	0
Nuttall's Cottontail	*Sylvilagus nuttallii*	1	1
White-tailed Jackrabbit	*Lepus townsendii*	0	0
Black-tailed Jackrabbit	*Lepus californicus*	1	1
Pygmy Rabbit	*Brachylagus idahoensis*	0	0
Least Chipmunk	*Tamias minimus*	0	0
Yellow-bellied Marmot	*Marmota flaviventris*	1	1
White-tailed Antelope Squirrel	*Ammospermophilus leucurus*	0	1
Fox Squirrel	*Sciurus niger*	1	1
Paiute Ground Squirrel	*Spermophilus mollis*	1	1
Belding's Ground Squirrel	*Spermophilus beldingi*	1	1
Townsend's Pocket Gopher	*Thomomys townsendii*	0	0
Northern Pocket Gopher	*Thomomys talpoides*	1	1
Great Basin Pocket Mouse	*Perognathus parvus*	1	1
Ord's Kangaroo Rat	*Dipodomys ordii*	1	1
Chisel-toothed Kangaroo Rat	*Dipodomys microps*	1	1
Western Harvest Mouse	*Reithrodontomys megalotis*	1	1
House Mouse	*Mus musculus*	1	1
Deer Mouse	*Peromyscus maniculatus*	1	1
Northern Grasshopper Mouse	*Onychomys leucogaster*	0	0
Desert Woodrat	*Neotoma lepida*	0	0
Bushy-tailed Woodrat	*Neotoma cinerea*	1	1
Montane Vole	*Microtus montanus*	1	1
Long-tailed Vole	*Microtus longicaudus*	1	0
Sagebrush Vole	*Lemmiscus curtatus*	1	1
Muskrat	*Ondatra zibethicus*	1	1
Porcupine	*Erethizon dorsatum*	1	1
Beaver	*Castor canadensis*	1	0

Table 2. List of mammal species expected or possible in the monument and their status during the 2003 inventory (continued).

Common Name	Scientific Name	Expected	Confirmed
Coyote	*Canis latrans*	1	1
Red Fox	*Vulpes vulpes*	1	1
Raccoon	*Procyon lotor*	1	1
Long-tailed Weasel	*Mustela frenata*	1	0
Mink	*Mustela vison*	1	0
Badger	*Taxidea taxus*	1	1
Spotted Skunk	*Spilogale gracilis*	1	0
Striped Skunk	*Mephitis mephitis*	1	1
River Otter	*Lutra canadensis*	1	0
Mountain Lion	*Felis concolor*	0	0
Bobcat	*Lynx rufus*	1	0
Mule Deer	*Odocoileus hemionus*	1	1
Pronghorn	*Antilocapra americana*	1	1
Total		**39**	**26**
Percent Confirmed			**0.67**
Total w/o bats		**33**	**26**
Percent Confirmed			**0.79**

Table 3. Location, trap type, and number of trap nights for mammal trap transects, miscellaneous trap locations, and Havahart trap locations in the monument during 2003.

Transect	Date	UTM X	UTM Y	Trap Nights	Trap Type
MISC01	4/10/03	670167	4736415	10	Sherman
TRAN01	4/10/03	670152	4736244	20	Sherman
TRAN02	4/10/03	670105	4736188	10	Sherman
TRAN03	4/10/03	666816	4737065	10	Sherman
TRAN04	4/10/03	666741	4737080	10	Sherman
TRAN05	5/19/03	670205	4736308	30	Sherman
MISC02	5/19/03	670379	4736257	10	Sherman
TRAN06	5/19/03	670383	4736192	20	Sherman
TRAN07	5/20/03	669925	4735976	20	Sherman
TRAN08	5/20/03	669748	4735972	20	Sherman
TRAN09	5/27/03	666555	4736895	30	Sherman
TRAN10	5/27/03	666519	4737010	30	Sherman
MISC03	5/28/03	668699	4742251	30	Sherman
TRAN11	5/28/03	668709	4742129	30	Sherman
TRAN12	5/31/03	668786	4741073	30	Sherman
MISC04	5/31/03	668913	4741441	30	Sherman
TRAN13	6/6/03	667040	4737326	20	Sherman
TRAN14	6/6/03	667119	4737066	20	Sherman
TRAN15	6/6/03	668653	4743555	20	Sherman
TRAN16	6/6/03	668704	4743542	20	Sherman
TRAN17	6/10/03	668856	4742476	30	Sherman
TRAN18	6/10/03	668414	4741942	30	Sherman
TRAN19	6/11/03	668853	4740984	20	Sherman
MISC05	6/11/03	668847	4741426	20	Sherman
TRAN20	6/22/03	668794	4741270	30	Sherman
MISC06	6/22/03	668969	4741023	30	Sherman
TRAN21	6/22/03	668548	4741522	30	Sherman
MISC08	6/22/03	667609	4741895	30	Sherman
TRAN22	7/1/03	668838	4742337	30	Sherman
TRAN23	7/1/03	668914	4742337	30	Sherman
MISC09	7/1/03	668584	4742453	30	Sherman
MISC10	7/1/03	669057	4747943	30	Sherman
MISC11	7/14/03	669253	4739971	20	Sherman
MISC12	7/14/03	668999	4739871	20	Sherman
MISC13	7/14/03	670168	4736296	20	Sherman
MISC14	8/17/03	670257	4735862	20	Sherman
MISC15	8/17/03	668969	4740764	20	Sherman
MISC16	8/17/03	668774	4740561	20	Sherman
HV01	8/1/03	668949	4742347	3	Havahart
HV03	8/1/03	668847	4740989	3	Havahart
HV04	8/1/03	666265	4738616	3	Havahart
HV05	8/17/03	668980	4740832	3	Havahart

Table 3. Location, trap type, and number of trap nights for mammal trap transects, miscellaneous trap locations, and Havahart trap locations in the monument during 2003 (continued).

Transect	Date	UTM X	UTM Y	Trap Nights	Trap Type
HV06	8/17/03	668803	4740537	3	Havahart
HV07	8/17/03	668710	4740607	3	Havahart
Total				**898**	

Table 4. Capture results and relative abundance of mammals based on 2003 capture efforts in the Hagerman National Fossil Beds NM.

Transect	PEMA	PEPA	MUMU	REMA	DIMI	DIOR	MIMO	Total
MISC01	3	0		2			1	5
TRAN01	6							6
TRAN02								0
TRAN03	1	2						3
TRAN04	6							6
TRAN05	9			1				10
MISC02	5							5
TRAN06	5			1				6
TRAN07	12							12
TRAN08	7			2				9
TRAN09	11	1						12
TRAN10	5							5
MISC03	10		1					11
TRAN11	5	1						6
TRAN12	2							2
MISC04	5		2					7
TRAN13	4							4
TRAN14	1							1
TRAN15	5							5
TRAN16	3	1						4
TRAN17	13		1					14
TRAN18	8							8
TRAN19	8							8
MISC05	5			2				7
TRAN20	3							3
MISC06	2			3				5
TRAN21	5	1		1				7
MISC08	14							14
TRAN22	8			1				9
TRAN23	11							11
MISC09	10							10
MISC10	2	1						3
MISC11	9							9
MISC12	10		1	1				12
MISC13								
MISC14								0
MISC15								0
MISC16								
Havaharts								

Table 4. Capture results and relative abundance of mammals based on 2003 capture efforts in the Hagerman National Fossil Beds NM (continued).

Transect	PEMA	PEPA	MUMU	REMA	DIMI	DIOR	MIMO	Total
HV01								0
HV02								0
HV03								0
HV04								0
HV05								0
HV06								0
HV07								0
Funnel Traps								
3								0
5								0
6	4							4
12	2			1				3
13	1							1
15	1	2						3
22		1						1
26								0
30	1	1						2
32								0
33	4	1		2				7
35	5	1				1		6
57	5	2		2			1	10
58								0
99	2	1						3
111A								0
122				3				3
157								0
187								0
196		1						1
225	3							3
254								0
629	3				3	1		7
700	1							1
720	3			1				4
756	1			1				2
960	1							1
989		1		1				2

Table 4. Capture results and relative abundance of mammals based on 2003 capture efforts in the Hagerman National Fossil Beds NM (continued).

Transect	PEMA	PEPA	MUMU	REMA	DIMI	DIOR	MIMO	Total
N1	1	1						2
N2								0
S1								0
S2								0
Total	**251**	**19**	**5**	**25**	**3**	**2**	**2**	**305**
Relative Abundance	**0.82**	**0.06**	**0.02**	**0.08**	**0.01**	**0.01**	**0.01**	

[a] PEMA= *Peromyscus maniculatus*   DIMI= *Dipodomys microps*
  PEPA= *Perognathus parvus*   DIOR= *Dipodomys ordii*
  MUMU= *Mus musculus*   MIMO= *Microtus montanus*
  REMA= *Reithrodontomys megalotis*

Table 5. List of expected and possible amphibian and reptile species and their confirmation status in the monument during the 2003 inventory.

Common Name	Scientific Name	Expected	Confirmed
Long-toed Salamander	*Ambystoma macrodactylum*	1	0
Tiger Salamander	*Ambystoma tigrinum*	0	0
Western Toad	*Bufo boreas*	1	1
Pacific Tree Frog	*Pseudacris regilla*	1	1
Western Chorus Frog	*Pseudacris maculata*	0	0
Great Basin Spadefoot	*Scaphiopus intermontanus*	1	1
Bullfrog	*Rana catsebeiana*	1	1
Northern Leopard Frog	*Rana pipiens*	1	0
Longnose Leopard Lizard	*Gambelia wislizenii*	1	0
Short-horned Lizard	*Phrynosoma douglasii*	0	0
Desert Horned Lizard	*Phrynosoma platyrhinos*	1	1
Sagebrush Lizard	*Sceloporus graciosus*	1	1
Western Fence Lizard	*Sceloporus occidentalis*	1	1
Side-blotched Lizard	*Uta stansburiana*	1	1
Great Basin Collared Lizard	*Crotaphytus bicinctores*	0	0
Western Skink	*Eumeces skiltonianus*	1	0
Western Whiptail	*Cnemidophorus tigris*	1	1
Rubber Boa	*Charina bottae*	0	0
Racer	*Coluber constrictor*	1	1
Striped Whipsnake	*Masticophis taeniatus*	1	1
Gopher Snake	*Pituophis catenifer*	1	1
Longnose Snake	*Rhinocheilus lecontei*	0	0
Western Ground Snake	*Sonora semiannulata*	0	0
Western Terrestrial Garter Snake	*Thamnophis elegans*	1	1
Western Rattlesnake	*Crotalus viridis*	1	1
Common Garter Snake	*Thamnophis sirtalis*	0	0
Night Snake	*Hypsiglena torquata*	0	0
Total		**18**	**14**
Percent Confirmed			**0.78**

Table 6. Locations, habitat type, slope, and aspect of amphibian and reptile traps during the 2003 vertebrate inventory in the Hagerman Fossil Beds NM.

Funnel Trap	UTM X	UTM Y	Habitat Type	Slope	Aspect
3	668443	4741653	Shrub	5-20	NE
5	668993	4740919	Riparian	0-5	Flat
6	666767	4736824	Shrub	5-20	SW
12	670205	4736308	Shrub	5-20	NE
13	668735	4741379	Riparian	5-20	NE
15	668765	4742290	Forest	0-5	Flat
22	667104	4737295	Shrub	5-20	SW
26	668814	4741609	Forest	5-20	SW
30	667274	4736480	Shrub	5-20	NE
32	668784	4741579	Forest	5-20	NE
33	668561	4743047	Shrub	5-20	NE
35	666535	4737196	Grassland	0-5	Flat
57	666674	4737059	Grassland	5-20	SW
58	668477	4742180	Shrub	5-20	SW
99	666341	4737020	Grassland	0-5	Flat
111A	670352	4736008	Riparian	0-5	Flat
122	666943	4736658	Shrub	0-5	Flat
157	667498	4742099	Grassland	0-5	Flat
187	667249	4742142	Grassland	0-5	Flat
196	668701	4743250	Riparian	5-20	SW
225	667602	4741688	Grassland	5-20	SW
254	668821	4742415	Riparian	0-5	Flat
629	666493	4736906	Grassland	5-20	SW
700	670363	4736044	Riparian	5-20	NE
720	670294	4735826	Riparian	0-5	Flat
756	670383	4736196	Riparian	5-20	NE
960	668731	4742185	Forest	0-5	Flat
989	668528	4743321	Riparian	5-20	SW
N1	668614	4743139	Shrub	5-20	SW
N2	668632	4740947	Shrub	5-20	SW
S1	669698	4735968	Shrub	5-20	SW
S2	666731	4736880	Shrub	5-20	SW

Table 7. Capture results and relative abundance of amphibians and reptiles based on 2003 capture efforts in the Hagerman National Fossil Beds NM.

Funnel Trap	PHPL	CNTI	UTST	COCO	PICA	MATA	CRVI	BUBO	SCIN	Totals
					Species[a]					
3		1			1					2
5								1		1
6		1								1
12		2		5						7
13										0
15				1						1
22		1								1
26		1		1						2
30										0
32				1						1
33		1								1
35	3				2					5
57	2	3		2						7
58										0
99								1		1
111A										0
122					2		1			3
157		5								5
187		1								1
196									1	1
225										0
254										0
629						1				1
700				2	1					3
720				2	1					3
756										0
960				1	1					2
989										0
N1		11	1							12
N2		2								2
S1		7								7
S2		2	2		1					5
Totals	**5**	**38**	**3**	**15**	**8**	**1**	**1**	**2**	**1**	**75**
Relative Abundance	**0.067**	**0.507**	**0.04**	**0.2**	**0.107**	**0.013**	**0.013**	**0.027**	**0.013**	

[a] PHPL= *Phrynosoma platyrhinos*   MATA= *Masticophis taeniatus*
CNTI= *Cnemidophorus tigris*   CRVI= *Crotalus viridis*
UTST= *Uta stansburiana*   BUBO= *Bufo boreas*
COCO= *Coluber constrictor*   SCIN= *Scaphiophus intermontanus*
PICA= *Pituophis catenifer*

Appendix B. Species Account

The next section of this report gives a brief description of each expected or unexpected but possible species for the Hagerman Fossil Beds National Monument. Birds, mammals, and herpetofauna are divided into expected and unexpected species. Species names are followed by a series of codes based on those in use by the NPSpecies database. The first code indicates park status, followed by species abundance, and species residency. The information presented here is based on the 2003 inventory results and contributions from the Hagerman Valley Christmas Bird Count and Thousand Springs Nature Conservancy Reserve bird list from 1992-1998. A key to the codes used after the species names are located on the following page.

NPSpecies Codes

Park Status

- **(P) Present:**
  Species occurrence in park is documented and assumed to be extant.
- **(H) Historic:**
  Species historical occurrence in the park is documented, but recent investigations indicate that the species is now probably absent.
- **(PP) Probably Present:**
  Park is within species range and contains appropriate habitat. Documented occurrences of the species in the adjoining region of the park give reason to suspect that it probably occurs within the park. The degree of probability may vary within this category, including species that range from common to rare.
- **(E) Encroaching**
  The species is not documented in the park, but is documented as being adjacent to the park and has potential to occur in the park.
- **(U) Unexpected:**
  Included for the park based on weak (unconfirmed) record or no evidence, giving minimal indication of the species occurrence in the park.
- **(FR) False Report:**
  Species previously reported to occur within the park, but current evidence indicates that the report was based on a misidentification, a taxonomic concept no longer accepted, or some other similar problem of interpretation.

Species Abundance

- **(A) Abundant:**
  <u>Animals:</u> *May be seen daily, in suitable habitat and season, and counted in relatively large numbers.*
  <u>Plants:</u> *Large number of individuals; wide ecological amplitude or occurring in habitats covering a large portion of the park.*
- **(C) Common:**
  <u>Animals:</u> *May be seen daily, in suitable habitat and season, but not in large numbers.*
  <u>Plants:</u> *Large numbers of individuals predictably occurring in commonly encountered habitats but not those covering a large portion of the park.*
- **(U) Uncommon:**
  <u>Animals:</u> *Likely to be seen monthly in appropriate season/habitat. May be locally common.*
  <u>Plants:</u> *Few to moderate numbers of individuals; occurring either sporadically in commonly encountered habitats or in uncommon habitats.*
- **(R) Rare:**
  <u>Animals:</u> *Present, but usually seen only a few times each year.*
  <u>Plants:</u> *Few individuals, usually restricted to small areas of rare habitat.*
- **(O) Occasional:**
  Occurs in the park at least once every few years, but not necessarily every year. Applicable to animals only.
- **(UNK) Unknown:**
  Abundance unknown.

Residency

- **(B) Breeder:**
  Population reproduces in the park.
- **(R) Resident:**
  A significant population is maintained in the park for more than two months each year, but it is not known to breed there.
- **(M) Migratory:**
  Migratory species that occurs in park approximately two months or less each year and does not breed there.
- **(V) Vagrant:**
  Park is outside of the species usual range.
- **(UNK) Unknown:**
  Residency status in park is unknown.

Birds

Expected Species

Common Loon *Gavia immer*	Present	U	M
Pied-billed Grebe *Podilymbus podiceps*	Present	C	UNK
Eared Grebe *Podiceps nigricollis*	Present	U	M
Western Grebe *Aechmophorus occidentalis*	Present	C	UNK
Clark's Grebe *Aechmophorus clarkii*	Present	C	UNK
American White Pelican *Pelecanus erythrorhynchos*	Present	C	R
Double-crested Cormorant *Phalacrocorax auritus*	Present	C	R
Great Blue Heron *Ardea herodias*	Present	C	B
Great Egret *Ardea alba*	Present	U	M
Black-crowned Night Heron *Nycticorax nycticorax*	Present	C	B
Turkey Vulture *Cathartes aura*	Present	U	UNK
Snow Goose *Chen caerulescens*	Present	R	M
Canada Goose *Branta canadensis*	Present	C	B
Tundra Swan *Cygnus columbianus*	Present	R	M
Wood Duck *Aix sponsa*	Present	U	UNK
Gadwall *Anas strepera*	Present	U	B
American Widgeon *Anas Americana*	Present	A	R
Mallard *Anas platyrhynchos*	Present	A	B
Blue-winged Teal *Anas discors*	Present	U	UNK
Cinnamon Teal *Anas cyanoptera*	Present	C	B
Northern Shoveler *Anas clypeata*	Present	C	UNK
Northern Pintail *Anas acuta*	Present	U	R

39

Green-winged Teal *Anas crecca*	Present	R	UNK
Canvasback *Aythya valisineria*	Present	U	R
Redhead *Aythya Americana*	Present	U	UNK
Ring-necked Duck *Aythya collaris*	Present	U	R
Lesser Scaup *Aythya affinis*	Present	C	UNK
Bufflehead *Bucephala albeola*	Present	C	R
Common Goldeneye *Bucephala clangula*	Present	C	R
Common Merganser *Mergus merganser*	Present	R	R
Hooded Merganser *Lophodytes cucullatus*	Present	R	R
Ruddy Duck *Oxyura jamaicensis*	Present	U	UNK
Osprey *Pandion haliaetus*	Present	U	B
Bald Eagle *Haliaetus leucocephalus*	Present	C	R
Northern Harrier *Circus cyaneus*	Present	C	B
Sharp-shinned Hawk *Accipiter striatus*	Present	R	R
Cooper's Hawk *Accipiter cooperii*	Present	R	R
Northern Goshawk *Accipiter gentiles*	Present	R	R
Swainson's Hawk *Buteo swainsoni*	Present	U	B
Red-tailed Hawk *Buteo jamaicensis*	Present	C	B
Ferruginous Hawk *Buteo regalis*	Present	U	B
Rough-legged Hawk *Buteo lagopus*	Present	R	R
Golden Eagle *Aquila chrysaetos*	Present	U	UNK
American Kestrel *Falco sparverius*	Present	C	B
Merlin *Falco columbarius*	Present	R	R

Peregrine Falcon *Falco peregrinus*	Present	R	M
Prairie Falcon *Falco mexicanus*	Present	U	UNK
Gray Partridge *Perdix perdix*	Present	U	B
Chukar *Alectoris chukar*	Present	U	B
Ring-necked Pheasant *Phasianus colchicus*	Present	C	B
California Quail *Callipepla californica*	Present	C	B
Virginia Rail *Rallus limicola*	Present	U	B
Sora *Porzana carolina*	Present	R	B
American Coot *Fulica americana*	Present	A	B
Killdeer *Charadrius vociferous*	Present	C	B
American Avocet *Recurvirostra americana*	Present	O	M
Spotted Sandpiper *Actitis macularia*	Present	U	M
Long-billed Curlew *Numenius americanus*	Present	R	UNK
Common Snipe *Gallinago gallinago*	Present	U	B
Wilson's Phalarope *Phalaropus tricolor*	Present	U	UNK
Franklin Gull *Larus pipixcan*	Present	R	M
Ring-billed Gull *Larus delawarensis*	Present	C	UNK
California Gull *Larus californicus*	Present	C	UNK
Herring Gull *Larus argentatus*	Present	R	R
Caspian Tern *Sterna caspia*	Present	U	M
Forster's Tern *Sterna forsteri*	Present	U	M
Rock Dove *Columba livia*	Present	A	B
Mourning Dove *Zenaida macroura*	Present	C	B

Barn Owl *Tyto alba*	Present	U	B	
Western Screech Owl *Otus kennicottii*	Present	U	B	
Great-horned Owl *Bubo virginianus*	Present	U	B	
Burrowing Owl *Athene cunicularia*	Present	R	B	
Long-eared Owl *Asio otus*	Present	R	R	
Short-eared Owl *Asio flammeus*	Present	R	UNK	
Common Nighthawk *Chordeiles minor*	Present	C	B	
Common Poorwill *Phalaenoptilus nuttallii*	Present	UNK	B	
Black-chinned Hummingbird *Archilochus alexandri*	Present	U	B	
Rufous Hummingbird *Selasphorous rufus*	Present	R	M	
Belted Kingfisher *Ceryle alcyon*	Present	C	B	
Downy Woodpecker *Picoides pubescens*	Present	U	B	
Hairy Woodpecker *Picoides villosus*	Present	R	R	
Northern Flicker *Colaptes auratus*	Present	C	B	
Western Wood Pewee *Contopus sordidulus*	Present	U	B	
Dusky Flycatcher *Empidonax oberholseri*	Present	R	M	
Gray Flycatcher *Empidonax wrightii*	Present	R	UNK	
Say's Phoebe *Sayornis saya*	Present	U	B	
Ash-throated Flycatcher *Myiarchus cinerascens*	Present	R	UNK	
Western Kingbird *Tyrannus verticalis*	Present	C	B	
Eastern Kingbird *Tyrannus tyrannus*	Present	U	B	
Loggerhead Shrike *Lanius ludovicianus*	Present	U	B	
Northern Shrike *Lanius excubitor*	Present	U	R	

Warbling Vireo *Vireo gilvus*	Probably Present		
Black-billed Magpie *Pica pica*	Present	A	B
American Crow *Corvus brachyrhyncos*	Present	C	B
Common Raven *Corvus corax*	Present	C	B
Horned Lark *Eremophila alpestris*	Present	U	B
Tree Swallow *Tachycineta bicolor*	Present	U	B
Violet-green Swallow *Tachycineta thalassina*	Present	U	B
Northern Rough-winged Swallow *Stelgidopteryx serripennis*	Present	U	B
Bank Swallow *Riparia riparia*	Present	U	B
Cliff Swallow *Petrochelidon pyrrhonata*	Present	C	B
Barn Swallow *Hirundo rustica*	Present	C	B
Black-capped Chickadee *Poecile atricapillus*	Present	U	R
Mountain Chickadee *Poecile gambeli*	Present	U	R
Bushtit *Psaltriparus minimus*	Present	U	R
Red-breasted Nuthatch *Sitta canadensis*	Present	U	R
Brown Creeper *Certhia americana*	Present	U	R
Rock Wren *Salpinctes obsoletus*	Present	U	B
Canyon Wren *Catherpes mexicanus*	Present	C	B
House Wren *Troglodytes aedon*	Present	R	B
Marsh Wren *Cistothorus palustris*	Present	C	B
American Dipper *Cinclus mexicanus*	Present	R	UNK
Golden-crowned Kinglet *Regulus satrapa*	Present	U	R
Ruby-crowned Kinglet *Regulus calendula*	Present	U	UNK

Mountain Bluebird *Sialia currucoides*	PresentR	R	
Townsend's Solitaire *Myadestes townsendi*	PresentU	R	
American Robin *Turdus migratorius*	Present	A	B
Sage Thrasher *Oreoscoptes montanus*	Present	U	B
European Starling *Sturnus vulgaris*	Present	A	B
American Pipit *Anthus rubescens*	Present	U	M
Bohemian Waxwing *Bombycilla garrulus*	Present	R	V
Cedar Waxwing *Bombycilla cedrorum*	Present	U	R
Orange-crowned Warbler *Vermivora celata*	Present	R	M
Yellow Warbler *Dendroica petechia*	Present	C	B
Yellow-rumped Warbler *Dendroica coronata*	Present	U	R
Wilson's Warbler *Wilsonia pusilla*	Present	U	M
Yellow-breasted Chat *Icteria virens*	Present	C	B
Western Tanager *Piranga ludoviciana*	Present	U	M
Green-tailed Towhee *Pipilo chlorurus*	Probably Present		
Spotted Towhee *Pipilo maculates*	Present	U	R
American Tree Sparrow *Spizella arborea*	Present	R	R
Chipping Sparrow *Spizella passerina*	Present	R	M
Brewer's Sparrow *Spizella breweri*	Present	R	B
Vesper Sparrow *Poocetes gramineus*	Present	R	B
Lark Sparrow *Chondestes grammacus*	Present	U	B
Sage Sparrow *Amphispiza belli*	Present	R	B
Savannah Sparrow *Passerculus sandwichensis*	Present	R	B

Fox Sparrow *Passerella iliaca*	Present	R	M	
Song Sparrow *Melospiza melodia*	Present	C	B	
Lincoln's Sparrow *Melospiza lincolnii*	Present	R	M	
White-crowned Sparrow *Zonotrichia leucophrys*	Present	C	R	
Dark-eyed Junco *Junco hyemalis*	Present	C	R	
Black-headed Grosbeak *Pheuticus melanocephalus*	Present	U	M	
Lazuli Bunting *Passerina amoena*	Present	U	B	
Red-winged Blackbird *Agelaius phoeniceus*	Present	C	B	
Western Meadowlark *Sturnella neglecta*	Present	C	B	
Yellow-headed Blackbird *Xanthocephalus xanthocephalus*	Present	C	B	
Brewer's Blackbird *Euphagus cyanocephalus*	Present	C	B	
Brown-headed Cowbird *Molothrus ater*	Present	U	B	
Bullock's Oriole *Icterus bullockii*	Present	U	B	
Cassin's Finch *Carpodacus cassinii*	Present	R	R	
House Finch *Carpodacus mexicanus*	Present	C	B	
Pine Siskin *Carduelis pinus*	Present	U	R	
American Goldfinch *Carduelis tristis*	Present	C	B	
Evening Grosbeak *Coccothraustes vespertinus*	Present	R	M	
House Sparrow *Passer domesticus*	Present	U	B	

Unexpected Species

Snowy Egret *Egretta thula*	Present	R	M	
Cattle Egret *Bubulcus ibis*	Present	R	M	

White-faced Ibis *Plegadis chihi*	Unexpected		
Ross's Goose *Chen rossii*	Unexpected		
Mute Swan *Cygnus olor*	Present	U	UNK
Eurasian Wigeon *Anas Penelope*	Present	R	R
Tufted Duck *Aythya fuligula*	Present	O	V
Greater Scaup *Aythya marila*	Present	R	M
Long-tailed Duck *Clangula hyemalis*	Present	O	V
Barrow's Goldeneye *Bucephala islandica*	Present	U	R
Red-breasted Merganser *Mergus serrator*	Present	R	M
Sage Grouse *Centrocercus urophasianus*	Unexpected		
Sandhill Crane *Grus canadensis*	Unexpected		
Black-bellied Plover *Pluvialis squatarola*	Unexpected		
Semipalmated Plover *Charadrius semipalmatus*	Unexpected		
Black-necked Stilt *Himantopus mexicanus*	Present	U	M
Greater Yellowlegs *Tringa melanoleuca*	Unexpected		
Lesser Yellowlegs *Tringa flavipes*	Unexpected		
Willet *Catoptrophorus semipalmatus*	Unexpected		
Marbled Godwit *Limosa fedoa*	Present	R	M
Sanderling *Calidris alba*	Present	R	M
Semipalmated Sandpiper *Calidris pusilla*	Present	R	M
Least Sandpiper *Calidris minutilla*	Present	U	M
Pectoral Sandpiper *Calidris melanotos*	Unexpected		
Short-billed Dowitcher *Limnodromus griseus*	Present	O	M

Long-billed Dowitcher *Limnodromus scolopaceus*	Present		R	M
Bonaparte's Gull *Larus philadelphia*	Present	U	M	
Mew Gull *Larus canus*	Unexpected			
Thayer's Gull *Larus thayeri*	Unexpected			
Glaucous Gull *Larus hyperboreas*	Unexpected			
Glaucous-winged Gull *Larus glaucescens*	Unexpected			
Common Tern *Sterna hirundo*	Present	R	M	
Black Tern *Childonias niger*	Present	R	M	
Northern Saw-whet Owl *Aegolius acadicus* Present			R	M
White-throated Swift *Aeronautes saxatalis* Present		U	M	
Calliope Hummingbird *Stellula calliope*	Present	R	M	
Broad-tailed Hummingbird *Selasphorus platycercus*	Present		O	M
Willow Flycatcher *Empidonax traillii*	Present	R		B
Hammond's Flycatcher *Empidonax hammondii*		Present	O	M
Cordilleran Flycatcher *Empidonax occidentalis*		Present	O	M
Red-eyed Vireo *Vireo olivaceus*	Present	R	M	
Stellar's Jay *Cyanocitta stelleri*	Present	R	M	
Blue Jay *Cyanocitta cristata*	Present	R	V	
Western Scrub Jay *Aphelocoma californica* Present		R	M	
White-breasted Nuthatch *Sitta canadensis* Present			R	UNK
Winter Wren *Troglodytes troglodytes*	Present	R	R	
Swainson's Thrush *Catharus ustulatus*	Unexpected			
Hermit Thrush *Catharus guttatus*	Present	R	M	

Varied Thrush *Ixoreus naevius*	Present	R	M	
Gray Catbird *Dumetella carolinensis*	Unexpected			
Northern Mockingbird *Mimus polyglottos*	Unexpected			
Bohemian Waxwing *Bombycilla garrulus*	Present	R	M	
MacGillivray's Warbler *Oporornis tolmiei*	Present	U	M	
Common Yellowthroat *Geothlypis trichas*	Present	U	M	
Grasshopper Sparrow *Ammodramus savannarum*	Present	R	UNK	
Golden-crowned Sparrow *Zonotrichia atricapilla*	Present	R	R	
Harris Sparrow *Zonotrichia querula*	Present	O	V	
Snow Bunting *Plecotrophenax nivalis*	Present	O	M	
Bobolink *Dolichonyx oryzivorus*	Unexpected			
Common Redpoll *Carduelis flammea*	Unexpected			
Lesser Goldfinch *Carduelis psaltria*	Unexpected			

Mammals

Expected Species

Vagrant Shrew *Sorex vagrans*   Probably Present

Mountain Cottontail *Sylvilagus nuttallii*   Present   C   B

The mountain cottontail occurs throughout the monument. This species was often seen in shrub habitat along roadsides.

Black-tailed Jackrabbit *Lepus californicus*   Present   C   B

This species was observed throughout the monument. The black-tailed jackrabbit was seen often in the morning or evening hours along roads.

Yellow-bellied Marmot *Marmota flaviventris*   Present   U   UNK

This species is found on the outskirts on the east portion of the monument and occurs mainly on the east side of the river where rock is more abundant. There is an abundance of melon grating of the basaltic rock along the east side of the Snake River.

Fox Squirrel *Sciurus niger*   Present   C   B

The fox squirrel occurred throughout the forest and riparian areas on both east and west portions of the monument. This included the Russian olive and cottonwood trees along the Snake River and the Yahoo Creek drainage.

Piute Ground Squirrel *Spermophilus mollis*   Present   U   B

This species occurred along the top of the monument along the road 400 E. Their burrows were located along the roads and across from agriculture fields.

Belding's Ground Squirrel *Spermophilus beldingi*   Present   U   B

This species occurred along the top of the monument along the road 400 E. Their burrows were located along the roads and across from agriculture fields.

Northern Pocket Gopher *Thomomys talpoides*   Present   C   B

The mounds and tunnels formed by the species were observed throughout the monument.

Great Basin Pocket Mouse *Perognathus parvus*   Present   C   B

The great basin pocket mouse occurs throughout the monument. This species was most often found in the shrub habitat. Funnel traps and Sherman traps were effective in capturing this species.

Chisled-toothed Kangaroo Rat *Dipodomys microps*   Present   U   B

This species was captured in the southern portion of the monument in funnel traps in sagebrush and open sandy soils.

Ord's Kangaroo Rat *Dipodomys ordii*   Present   U   B

This species occurs throughout the monument. It was captured along the Emigrant hiking trail in funnel traps. The species is associated with loose sandy soils.

Beaver *Castor canadensis*   Probably Present

Western Harvest Mouse *Reithrodontomys microps*   Present   C   B

This species was captured throughout the monument and typically found in grassy areas and among dead Russian thistle piles.

Deer Mouse *Peromyscus maniculatus*   Present   A   B

This species is abundant and was captured throughout the monument. Trapping locations were varied habitats, with which included grasslands, woodlands, brush areas, and in riparian areas.

House Mouse *Mus musculus*   Present   U   B

The house mouse was captured in the disturbed forest areas along the Snake River. These areas mainly consisted of Russian olive, cottonwood, cheatgrass, and debris.

Bushy-tailed Woodrat *Neotoma cinerea*   Present   U   B

This species was located on the small outcropping of basalt rock near the seeps and along the forested gulleys on the north end of the monument. The bushy-tailed woodrat was confirmed by incidental observations. One specimen was confirmed from skeletal remains.

Montane Vole *Microtus montanus*   Present   U   B

The montane vole was found in brushy and forested habitats. It was captured in both the Sherman and the funnel traps. This species was captured more frequently after rainfall.

Long-tailed Vole *Microtus longicaudus*   Probably Present

Sagebrush Vole *Lemmiscus curtatus*   Present   R   B

This species was captured during small mammal surveys conducted by Idaho Power in 1995.

Muskrat *Ondatra zibethicus*   Present   C   B

This species was often seen along the sides of the Snake River at dusk. Burrows were found in cattail stands.

Porcupine *Erethizon dorsatum*   Present   R   B

This species was observed once in the north section of the monument at dusk. The porcupine was found at the beginning of the inventory.

River Otter *Lutra canadensis*   Probably Present

Coyote *Canis latrans*   Present   C   B

The coyote was observed throughout the monument. It was often seen at dawn and dusk. Incidental observations, calls, scat, and tracks were found in both the north and the south section of the monument.

Red Fox *Vulpes vulpes*   Present   U   B

This species was observed in the north section of the monument. It was seen along the one of the bluffs. The red fox has also been seen by monument staff in recent years.

Raccoon *Procyon lotor*   Present   U   B

This species was observed in and adjacent to the monument. More often they were seen on the east side of the monument. The raccoon was often seen dead along Highway 30. This species was also confirmed by incidental observation by monument staff.

Long-tailed Weasel *Mustela erminea*   Probably Present

Mink *Mustela vison*   Probably Present

Spotted Skunk *Spilogale gracilis*   Probably Present

Striped Skunk *Mephitis mephitis*   Present   U   B

The striped skunk was found on both the east and west sections of the monument. Many individuals were found dead along highway 30 on the way to the monument.

Bobcat *Lynx rufus*   Probably Present

Mule Deer *Odocoileus hemionus*   Present   C   B

The mule deer was confirmed by incidental observations in the north and south sections of the national monument. This species was frequently seen in forested habitats and among the seeps on the bluffs.

Pronghorn *Antilocapra americana*   Present   R   UNK

The pronghorn was seen on the outskirts of the monument in one of the alfalfa fields on the top of the monument bluff. This species was only observed once.

Unexpected Species

Merriam's Shrew *Sorex merriami*   Unexpected

This species may occur in the monument but is very difficult to capture.

White-tailed Jackrabbit *Lepus townsendii* Unexpected

This species is rare throughout its range and generally occurs in areas of more extensive grasslands than what are available in the monument (Verts and Carraway 1998, Digital Atlas of Idaho 2003).

Pygmy Rabbit *Brachylagus idahoensis*   Unexpected

This species requires special soil and vegetation conditions and is rare throughout its range and is not thought to occur in the Hagerman Valley (Rachlow and Svancara 2003). The species is listed as a species of special concern in Idaho.

Least Chipmunk *Tamias minimus*   Unexpected

This conspicuous and diurnal species occurs in sagebrush habitat similar to that found in the monument but was never been documented there. It is unlikely to occur there.

White-tailed Antelope Squirrel *Ammosphermophilus leucurus*   Present UNK UNK

This species was captured along the Emigrant Trail in a funnel trap. This was located near access point 2 in the south section in the shrub habitat. The documentation of this species in Hagerman Fossil Beds represents a modest eastward range extension by approximately 40 miles.

Townsend's Pocket Gopher *Thomomys townsendii*   Unexpected

This species is poorly known in Idaho (Digital Atlas of Idaho 2003). The species may occur in or near the Hagerman Valley but specific trapping for pocket gophers needs to be conducted in the monument.

Northern Grasshopper Mouse *Onychomys leucogaster*   Unexpected

This species may occur in the monument but is very difficult to capture (Verts and Carraway 1998, Digital Atlas of Idaho 2003). However, the absence of the species during use of funnel traps and pitfalls in 2003 further indicates that the species may not occur in the monument.

Desert Woodrat *Neotoma lepida*   Unexpected

This species is poorly known in Idaho (Larrison 1982, Digital Atlas of Idaho 2003). The species may occur in or near the Hagerman Valley but the lack of rocky habitat may preclude the species from the area.

Mountain Lion *Puma concolor*   Unexpected

This species may occur sporadically in the monument but is very difficult to detect.

Amphibians amd Reptiles

Expected Species

Long-toed Salamander *Ambystoma macrodactylum*   Probably Present

Western Toad *Bufo boreas*   Present   C   B

This species was found along the Snake River and in other riparian areas. The western toad was also captured in funnel traps.

Pacific Treefrog *Pseudacris regilla*   Present   U   B

This species was heard along the banks of the river at dusk.

Great Basin Spadefoot Toad *Scaphiopus intermontanus*   Present   U   B

The great basin spadefoot toad was found in funnel traps along the Snake River. This species was also confirmed near a seep close to the irrigation plant.

Northern Leopard Frog *Rana pipiens*   Probably Present

Bullfrog *Rana catesbeiana*   Present   A   B

The bullfrog was seen and heard along the Snake River. This species was found on the both the east and the west sides of the monument.

Long-nosed Leopard Lizard *Gambelia wislizenii*   Probably Present

Desert Horned Lizard *Phrynosoma platyrhinos*   Present   C   B

The desert horned lizard was seen throughout the monument, but the majority was caught in the south section along the trail at access point two. This species was found in shrub habitats and among loose open soils. Ants are the majority of the horned lizard's diet and the abundance of ant mounds offered many foraging opportunities.

Sagebrush Lizard *Sceloporus graciosus*   Present   R   B

Only one of these species was found on the monument. It was found near the fossil butte and pitfall N1. This area was characterized by shrub habitat with open soil and a southwest-facing slope.

Western Fence Lizard *Sceloporus occidentalis*   Present   U   B

This species was often seen on the outskirts of the monument on the melon grating basaltic rocks or on fence posts.

Side-blotched Lizard *Uta stansburiana*   Present   C   B

The side-blotched lizard occurred throughout the monument. This species was often caught in the funnel traps.

Western Skink *Eumeces skiltonianus*   Probably Present

Western Whiptail *Cnemidophorus tigris*   Present   A   B

This was the most commonly seen lizard on the monument. The funnel traps were very effective in the capture of this species. The western whiptail was commonly found in the shrub habitats.

Racer *Coluber constrictor*   Present   C   B

Funnel traps were the most effective way the find this species. The racer was found in both sections of the Hagerman Fossil Beds, usually in either the forest or the shrub habitats.

Striped Whipsnake *Masticophis taeniatus*   Present   U   B

This species was seen in the shrub habitats in the north section on top of and below the bluffs. In the north section it was observed amongst shale along the bluffs. In the southern section the species was observed on a southwest facing slope in shrub and open soil habitat.

Gopher Snake *Pituophis catenifer*   Present   A   B

This was the most abundant snake species found on the monument. It was located on both the east and the west side of the river. The gopher snake was observed in all four of the habitat categories.

Western Terrestrial Garter Snake *Thamnophis elegans*   Present   R   UNK

The western terrestrial garter snake was observed on the east side of the monument outside the paleontologist lab on the gravel road at dusk. This was found near an irrigation canal that runs through this section.

Western Rattlesnake *Crotalus viridis*   Present   C   B

This species was observed throughout the monument. The western rattlesnake was often observed along the rivers edge in the riparian areas and in shrubs habitats. Other times they were observed along the hiking trails of both the north and south sections. Many individuals were found dead along the roads.

Unexpected Species

Tiger Salamander *Ambystoma tigrinum*   Unexpected

The predicted range of this species does not include the Hagerman Valley (Digital Atlas of Idaho 2003).

Western Chorus Frog *Pseudacris maculate*   Unexpected

The predicted range of this species does not include the Hagerman Valley (Digital Atlas of Idaho 2003).

Short-horned Lizard *Phrynosoma douglassi*   Unexpected

The predicted range of this species does not include the Hagerman Valley (Digital Atlas of Idaho 2003).

Great Basin Collard Lizard *Crotaphytus bicinctores*   Unexpected

While this species may occur in or near the Hagerman Valley, it is not expected in the monument due to the lack of significant rocky habitats (Digital Atlas of Idaho 2003).

Rubber Boa *Charina bottea*   Unexpected

This range of this species may not include the Hagerman Valley and the habitat requirements of the species may not be met in the monument (Digital Atlas of Idaho 2003).

Longnose Snake *Rhinocheilus lecontei*   Unexpected

The predicted range of this species does not include the Hagerman Valley (Digital Atlas of Idaho 2003).

Western Ground Snake *Sonora semiannulata*   Unexpected

The predicted range of this species does not include the Hagerman Valley (Digital Atlas of Idaho 2003).

Common Garter Snake *Thamnophis sirtalis fitchi* Probably Present

The predicted range of this species does not include the Hagerman Valley (Digital Atlas of Idaho 2003).

Night Snake *Hypsiglena torquata*   Probably Present

The predicted range of this species does not include the Hagerman Valley (Digital Atlas of Idaho 2003).

NPS 300/101467, March 2010